Wealth & Piety

Endorsements

Warning: This book could change your life. Can a comfortable person and a poor person be friends? What do Middle Easterners think about that? What does the Bible teach? Rich and surprising findings, with practical applications, drawing on thirty interviews and a lifetime of relationships. Thought-provoking and maybe game-changing. Read at your own risk!

Miriam Adeney, PhD
associate professor of World Christian Studies, Seattle Pacific University
author, *Daughters of Islam: Building Bridges with Muslim Women*

Karen Shaw has done a great service not only to expatriate workers but to us as national Christian leaders who are also often perceived, in times of crisis, as having "outside resources" to fall back on which the "normal" national Christian does not have! "Faith" takes on a different dimension in those who only have God to fall back on! May this book contribute to a deeper understanding of the relation between Christian faith, wealth, and true piety!

Ramez Atallah
general director, The Bible Society of Egypt

Karen Shaw's timely teaching should be carefully studied, discussed, and implemented by we believers whose natural inclinations—supported and sustained by our society's self-serving interests and its demonstrable capacity for self-deception—have been lulled into being mere *hearers* of God's word on mammon, but not doers, deceiving our own selves. I will read and recommend this small book again and again.

Jonathan J. Bonk, PhD
research professor of mission, Boston University
author, *Missions and Money: Affluence as a Western Missionary Problem*

This book is a timely contribution to the missiological literature on wealth and righteousness in a cross-cultural context. It is also a practical guide for effective mission in the Middle-East: Perceptions do matter even when one's own Western culture says otherwise. Dr. Shaw has earned the right to share these valuable insights as she has been immersed in Lebanese and Middle Eastern culture for many years.

Nabil Costa
CEO of the Lebanese Society for Educational and Social Development

---

Do you want to honor Christ with your money? Read this book! Do you **not** want to honor Christ with your money? Even more urgently, read this book! The biblical exploration of what it means to be both rich and righteous will open your heart and your purse. The insights from the Middle East will give you a fresh perspective on your own culture and its handling of money, and will also shed even more light on the Bible. Wherever you live in the world, read this book!

Ida Glaser
director emerita and international academic coordinator of the
Centre for Muslim-Christian Studies, Oxford

This is one of the most important books on money, morality, and the Christian spiritual life ever written. Its insight into Middle Eastern perspectives is especially valuable. Karen Shaw helps us delve deeply into biblical perspectives, then offers us an astonishing range of Middle Eastern wisdom on wealth and piety, and associated themes such as patronage, generosity, hospitality, appearance, God's sovereignty, relationships between rich and poor, spiritual friendship, and family life. The book is a wonder, and one that I will consult regularly and treasure.

Graham Hill, PhD
author, *GlobalChurch*

This is a book that will open your eyes on new insights on wealth and piety, allowing the Bible to speak to our daily life. Dr. Shaw challenges the reader through sharing life stories from the Middle East and offering practical advice. When you think about money in the life of the church, this book is a great resource.

Rev. Najla Kassab
president of the World Communion of Reformed Churches

Wealth and Piety leads us through one of the most profound and complex aspects of life and witness in the Middle East. Karen's mix of careful listening, probing questions, biblical reflection and gentle yet insightful critique is the fruit of many years in the region, and models exactly what we look for in cross-cultural workers. This will be high on our list of reading both for those who come and those who prepare them.

Canon Mike Parker
SIM Middle East Director SIM Middle East (formerly MECO)

Starting from a Biblical survey of the "righteous rich," Dr. Shaw leads us into a conversation with Middle Easterners around this very subject. The unique opportunity she gives us for reflection and then self-reflection is invaluable. A must read for not only the newly arrived expatriate but also for those with decades of experience. I only wish this book had been available when I first moved to the Middle East.

Grant Porter, PhD
program director, Cornerstone Trust long-term resident of the Middle East

Wealth & Piety

Middle Eastern Perspectives for Expat Workers

Karen L. H. Shaw

WILLIAM CAREY
PUBLISHING

Wealth and Piety: Middle Eastern Perspectives for Expat Workers
© 2018 by Karen L. H. Shaw

All rights reserved.

No part of this book may be reproduced, stored in a retrieval system, or transmitted in any form or by any means—electronic, mechanical, photocopy, recording, or otherwise—without prior written permission of the publisher, except brief quotations used in connection with reviews in magazines or newspapers. For permission, email permissions@wclbooks.com.

Scriptures are taken from the NEW INTERNATIONAL VERSION (NIV): Scripture taken from THE HOLY BIBLE, NEW INTERNATIONAL VERSION ®. Copyright© 1973, 1978, 1984, 2011 by Biblica, Inc.™ Used by permission of Zondervan.

Scripture quotations marked "ESV" are from The ESV® Bible (The Holy Bible, English Standard Version®), copyright © 2001 by Crossway, a publishing ministry of Good News Publishers. Used by permission. All rights reserved.

Published by William Carey Publishing
(formerly known as William Carey Library Publishers)
10 W. Dry Creek Cir | Littleton, CO 80120
www.missionbooks.org

William Carey Publishing is a ministry of Frontier Ventures
1605 E. Elizabeth St | Pasadena, CA 91104
www.frontierventures.org

Melissa Hicks, managing editor
Carla Foote, copyeditor
Mike Riester, cover design
Kathy Curtis and Mike Riester, interior design

Printed for Worldwide Distribution
23 22 21 20 19   IN

Library of Congress Cataloging-in-Publication Data

Names: Shaw, Karen L. H., author.
Title: Wealth and piety: Middle Eastern perspectives for expat workers / by Karen L.H. Shaw.
Description: Littleton: William Carey Publishing Publishing, 2018. | Includes bibliographical references. |
Identifiers: LCCN 2018034910 (print) | LCCN 2018036062 (ebook) |
  ISBN 9780878080809 (mobi) | ISBN 9780878080816 (epub) | ISBN 9780878080793 (print)
Subjects: LCSH: Missions to Muslims. | Wealth—Religious aspects—Christianity. | Wealth—Biblical teaching. | Missions—Middle East.
Classification: LCC BV2625 (ebook) | LCC BV2625 .S473 2018 (print) | DDC 266.00956—dc23
LC record available at https://lccn.loc.gov/2018034910

Dedication

To my precious parents,
Frederick Sherman Hull
and
Phyllis Lorraine Owen Hull
who taught me in word and action:
contentment,
the love of God,
the provision of God,
the joy of giving in Jesus' name,
and
the adventure of holding all of life as a loan from God.

Contents

Dedication	ix
Foreword by Timothy C. Tennent, PhD	xv
Acknowledgments	xvii
Introduction	xix
Definition of Terms and Language	xxii
You Can't Do Everything!	xxiii
1. The Righteous Rich in the Old Testament	1
Abraham: Our Rich, Righteous Father	1
Job: Permanently Righteous, Temporarily Rich	4
Deuteronomy	12
Solomon	19
The Proverbs	23
The Unrighteous Rich and Amos	27
2. The Righteous Rich in the New Testament	31
Righteousness and Riches in the Sermon on the Mount	31
The Acts of the Apostles and the Church in Jerusalem	39
James and the Unrighteous Rich	44
The Righteous Rich in 1 Timothy	48
Conclusion	55
Introducing the Interviewees	57

3. **Righteousness, Wealth, and Teaching Morality to Children** — **59**
    Teaching Morality to Children — 59
    Child-rearing, Godliness, and Wealth — 60
    Economic Piety: What and How Do Families Teach? — 63
    Middle Eastern Child-rearing, Wealth, Righteousness, and the Bible — 68
    Teaching Children Morality in Practice — 70

4. **Praising God and Acknowledging His Sovereignty** — **73**
    Praise, Sovereignty, and the Bible — 82
    Praise and God's Sovereignty in Practice — 84

5. **Generosity** — **87**
    Giving to God — 88
    Generosity to Family — 88
    Hospitality — 89
    Helping the Poor — 90
    Giving and the Honor of the Recipient — 91
    Class and Generosity — 93
    Motives for Giving — 94
    Giving and the Wider Causes of Poverty — 95
    Generosity and the Bible — 98
    Giving in Practice — 99

6. **Money: Where Did It Come From?** — **103**
    The Source of Wealth and the Bible — 116
    The Source of Money in Practice — 117

7. **Appearances** — **121**
    The Appearance of Less Wealth — 121
    The Appearance of Greater Wealth — 124
    Appearances and the Bible — 132
    Appearances in Practice — 134

8.	**Friendship between Rich and Poor**	**139**
	Barriers to Friendship between Poor and Rich	139
	Possibilities of Friendship	145
	What the Poor Want from the Rich	146
	The Bible and Friendship Between Rich and Poor	148
	Friendship in Practice	148
9.	**Patrons and Clients**	**151**
	An Introduction to the Patron-Client Relationship	151
	The Relationship Between Patron and Client	154
	Advantages of Patronage	157
	Disadvantages of Patronage	158
	The Righteous Patron	161
	Men of Religion and Patronage	166
	Patronage and the Bible	170
	Patronage in Practice	172

Epilogue	**183**
Glossary	**185**
Bibliography	**187**

Foreword

Behind Karen Shaw's valuable book lies the important, but often neglected fact that the proclamation of the gospel happens not merely in well-crafted words and doctrinally precise statements, but in and through our embodied presence in the world. So, it is truly a gift that Karen Shaw has identified one of the deepest challenges cross-cultural workers from the West face: How to navigate the perceptions and obligations which are rooted in wealth disparity between ourselves and those whom we serve. Not since Jonathan Bonk's landmark book, *Missions and Money*, which dropped like a bombshell on the church, has someone taken up the challenge of that book and applied it so powerfully and poignantly to their particular context in the Middle East.

Drawing from nearly three decades of living and working in the Middle East, Karen Shaw has taken time to listen deeply to men and women of the region. Her insights simply cannot be found in the myriad of traditional books that are used to prepare people for cross-cultural service. Yet, this issue regularly emerges in many regions of the world. Most cross-cultural workers from the West see themselves as sacrificially poor. They have given up potential lucrative careers in their homeland. They often have to raise their own support to do ministry. They have many financial pressures related to their children's education, and so forth. Yet, the deep reality is that in both perception and reality, we remain rich in comparison with the majority of the world's peoples. Dr. Shaw's questionnaires and thirty-five in-depth interviews have helped to capture these perceptions and, in the process, provides enormous guidance in how we are to live as the righteous rich. She focuses on the Middle East, but her insights would be of enormous value to cross-cultural workers around the world.

The other great value of *Middle Eastern Perspectives on Wealth and Piety* is its rootedness in the biblical text. The author faithfully examines many key passages from both Old and New Testaments that explore the theme of money and possessions. Her ability to synthesize the teachings of the Scriptures on this topic is remarkable. Building on that foundation, the entire work serves as a contextual bridge that takes the revelation of the Word of God and applies it faithfully to the local setting. In the end, you will gain many valuable insights into the nature of wealth, the way it influences relationships, and how piety and patronage are understood in much of the world.

If this book is read carefully, it may well produce the kind of relational renaissance that has heretofore eluded us in the Middle East and beyond. I heartily commend this study to you and am eager to see these insights shared with the wider church.

Timothy C. Tennent, PhD
professor of World Christianity
president, Asbury Theological Seminary

Acknowledgments

My heartfelt thanks to the thirty-five people who patiently and helpfully answered a long series of questions in individual and group interviews. The names of most of them can be found between chapters two and three. Many of the interviewees also modeled for me the gracious hospitality of which they spoke. I have learned much from them. They are the true authors: I merely summarized their thoughts. A special thanks to Emad and Almaz for hosting and finding two additional interviewees for the Egyptian gathering, and to Abu Nader for taking a day off work to help a total stranger.

As part of my initial study, I included a written survey, and I am grateful to the 190 people who took the time to complete it, along with a number of friends who oversaw distribution and collection of the surveys for me. I am especially grateful to Steph Christiansen for her zeal in getting more than 100 of the 190 samples.

I've been blessed with the help of some fine scholars. Dr. Jonathan Bonk's advice provided me with the goal and basic structure of this book. Dr. Diane King was eager to share her expertise, coach me in handling the crisis that accompanied my original study, and direct me to explore the nature of patronage. This book would have been a poorer product by far had it not been for her guidance. I am grateful to Dr. Tim Tennant, my doctoral supervisor, for his direction and suggestions for improvement. Some of my Arab Baptist Theological Seminary faculty colleagues also stimulated my thinking and encouraged me through their participation with me in our "study hall for faculty."

A huge thank you to my editors. Helen Parker is one of those amazing people who enjoys fixing grammar and obliterating obfuscation. She generously did the preliminary copy editing for me. I am grateful for Bob Heaton's editing skills and the hours he spent getting the manuscript up to scratch. Melissa Hicks and all of the diligent workers at William Carey Publishing, thank you!

It is entirely the fault of my wonderful husband, Dr. Perry Shaw, that this book is being published. He found my original research and, convinced it was too valuable to sit in an obscure file on my computer, proposed the book to William Carey Publishing. He then accomplished the feat of talking me into agreeing to the project. Perry has been my chief adviser and number one cheerleader as I updated and expanded the research and wrote the book. Also cheering me on have been our son, Chris, and our daughter, Phoebe.

In the course of interviewing and writing I have been reminded repeatedly of the lavish generosity of God whose gifts to this undeserving daughter are far too many to list here, but include all the ingredients of this book. Above all, to him I give eternal thanks.

Introduction

For many years, I have been vaguely uneasy about money. As a Western missionary living in the Middle East, I have received mixed and apparently contradictory signals from the society around me about lifestyle and money. It has been unsettling to be part of a society in which people hide behind showy facades and yet feel free to ask bluntly, "How much do you earn, and where does it come from?" Few believers in the region, whether foreign or local, can articulate a coherent theology of money and lifestyle. Advice from the missionary community is varied and conflicting, and often represents personal preferences or budgetary restrictions more than solid biblical and missiological thinking. The issue reached crisis proportions for me when I was living in one of the most exclusive areas of Beirut and serving in one of the city's most destitute shantytowns.

I had not realized the extent of my confusion with regard to wealth issues in Middle Eastern missions until I read *Missions and Money: Affluence as a Western Missionary Problem* by Jonathan Bonk.[1] Bonk notes that, in most places around the world, Western missionaries are perceived as wealthy by local people, regardless of their lifestyles or their self-perception.[2] In my experience, this is a true generalization for the Middle East, a few exceptions notwithstanding. People cannot fail to notice the fact that we travel, put our children in good schools, afford medical care, and have rich connections by local standards. Wade, who lived in Yemen, told me, "Even if you live in a slum, you're still rich." Nivin from Upper Egypt described the missionary as "having a lot of money in his pocket."

---

[1] Jonathan J. Bonk, *Missions and Money: Affluence as a Western Missionary Problem* (Orbis, Maryknoll, 1991).
[2] Ibid. xvii.

You protest. Naturally. Few people like to be told they are rich. We sense inherently that wealth implies obligation: "From everyone who has been given much, much will be demanded; and from the one who has been entrusted with much, much more will be asked."[3] We compare our incomes and lifestyles with our friends back home, or with what we might have had if we stayed home, and we feel virtuously deprived. Yet we will never convince the majority of our Middle Eastern acquaintances other than that we are rich.

A visit in the summer of 2004 with Dr. Bonk at the Overseas Ministries Study Center propelled me to take on the study you are now reading. Dr. Bonk urged me to answer my own questions in a wholesome missiological manner by addressing them first to the Scriptures, and then to the society in which I live. Specifically, he suggested that I consider the idea of "the righteous rich" in dialogue with both the Sacred Text and the cultural context of my ministry. In one of his articles Bonk declares, "We are in dire need of a theology of the righteous rich," and goes on to describe what that theology might look like in these terms:

> The role of the "righteous rich" as understood by the local community must inform the missionary's behavior. How do the poor among whom one lives distinguish between the unrighteous and the righteous rich? Affluent missionaries will need to learn to fulfill the obligations associated with the righteous rich as understood by his poor neighbors and colleagues. . . . It is nevertheless also true that at times what the Bible calls us to be and do falls short of human expectations. Jesus is our example here. He refused to fulfill the false expectations associated in the Jewish mind with the role of messiah, instead choosing the way of weakness, vulnerability, and the cross.[4]

The outline of this book follows the approach suggested by Bonk. Chapters one and two consist of studies of selected portions of

---

[3] Luke 12:48. All biblical quotations are from the New International Version (NIV), 1983 revision, unless otherwise noted.
[4] Jonathan J. Bonk, "Toward Common Sense Missiology: A Response," *Evangelical Missions Quarterly* 38:1, January (2002), 22–23.

Scripture and what they have to say about riches and godliness. This is not an attempt to mine everything the Scriptures have to say on the matter. Instead, I have presented what I hope is a representative sample of God's guidance regarding wealth and righteousness.

Chapters three to nine give us an opportunity to listen to what Middle Easterners have to say about wealth and piety, based on a series of qualitative interviews with over thirty representatives of nine Middle Eastern countries, either singly or in groups. Each of these chapters reflects on a key issue arising from the interviews, supplemented by occasional insights from a written survey of 190 Lebanese on the subject of wealth and piety which I conducted in 2005. Seven themes came up repeatedly:
1. the importance of child-rearing in developing wealth-related piety
2. the habit of praising God and acknowledging His sovereignty
3. giving to the poor as an essential characteristic of the righteous rich
4. the source of one's wealth and its relation to piety
5. the possibility (or otherwise) of a friendship between rich and poor
6. the role of appearances in attitudes toward wealth
7. patronage as a characteristic of the righteous rich.

Each of these concerns has implications for the lifestyle and ministry of Western Christian workers in the Middle East. In chapters three to nine, I present a detailed analysis of what the interviewees said, a brief look at how the views expressed by the interviewees compare with biblical teaching, and implications for foreign Western workers serving in the Middle East.

Definition of Terms and Language

It is customary to begin by defining terms, but for my purposes, to define terms at the start would be to miss the point entirely. The shape of the book is a pilgrimage, seeking first to discover how God understands the concept of "the righteous rich," based on his self-expression in the Scriptures, and then to discover how Middle Easterners perceive the same idea. In this way comparisons and contrasts can be made, and Middle Eastern views and our own brought under the commendation and condemnation of divine wisdom.

Few people like to be told they are rich.

However, a few initial comments about meanings are in order. "Rich" is relative. Job may not have had running water or electricity, but he was rich. In a written survey I conducted, Lebanese respondents identified signs of being rich ranging from having billions of dollars to owning three dogs. The difficulty of defining "rich" is further complicated in the region by the common practice of disguising one's economic status either upward or downward, depending on the country and the motivation. As a basic working definition, the second definition in the Shorter Oxford Dictionary is helpful: "Having large possessions or abundant means,"[5] if we add, "in comparison to other members of the same society." Some interviewees were quick to point out that true wealth is not primarily in material possessions, but for the sake of this study, "rich" will refer to the material realm unless otherwise noted.

I have chosen to accept the economic self-definitions of the interviewees such as "middle-class," "poor," "comfortable," and the like. The three-tiered class structure—rich, middle, poor—is widely accepted in the region, but the understanding of the boundaries between classes throughout the region is fuzzy in the extreme.

When it comes to "righteousness," the difficulty in finding a precise definition is made labyrinthine by the diverse linguistic, cultural, and historical sources of this study. Rather than attempt to reduce this Babel to one exact meaning, it seemed wiser to me to suggest a range of meanings and draw attention to the way the word is being used at any given time.

But what Arabic word to use? *Birr*, "righteousness" to Arab Christians, is only vaguely familiar to Muslims as a legal term. After consultation with several Arab friends, I chose to use the word *taqwā*, "piety," as the closest word in current usage to the biblical word "righteousness" common across sectarian boundaries. Ṭaqwā has general religious overtones which can be emphasized or de-emphasized and interpreted in either a sectarian or non-sectarian manner. Although I have translated the word as "piety," for most

---

[5] *The Shorter Oxford English Dictionary*, s. v. "Rich" (Clarendon, Oxford, 1973), p.1828.

Arabs the Arabic word does not carry the connotations of archaic rigidity that many English speakers now attach to "pious" and "piety." The interviewees' responses satisfied me that I had chosen the best word possible to provide freedom of expression within wide boundaries. Their responses give clues to how all sorts of typical missionary activities are perceived, from evangelism to conducting relief and development projects, and from relating to local pastors to befriending a beggar.

Arabic presents a particular challenge to gender neutrality, and the interviewees made no effort to use gender-inclusive language. It was my goal to give Middle Easterners their own voice, so, despite my personal preference, I have faithfully recorded and written using the masculine singular pronouns in a generic sense.

In translating and transcribing the interviews, I have sought to remain thoroughly accurate to the speaker's intention while smoothing over stilted language, grammatical errors, and redundancies. I did this both to present the interviewees' answers in their best light and to make reading their words smoother and more enjoyable.

You Can't Do Everything!
There are gaps in this study, yet there is a great deal of shared common culture which will make this study beneficial to anyone living in the region of the Middle East and North Africa, and probably to many other societies in which Islam or concerns for honor and shame predominate. Only nine Middle Eastern countries were directly represented by the interviewees. The very wealthy did not get a hearing. In seeking to represent the cultural norms of the majority, I was forced to neglect ethnic minorities living long-term in the region, such as Armenians, Gypsies, Kurds, and Turkmen. The distinctive culture of the Bedouins isn't discussed in these pages. Refugees are marginal to the study despite heartbreaking mass displacements. For me personally, the saddest omission is the hundreds of thousands of Asians, Africans, and Eastern Europeans who work in the region as domestics, laborers, and service industry personnel, or who are trafficked as slave labor or prostitutes. They are mentioned in the interviews only as "Chinese people" (sic.), household status symbols,

and inadequate replacements for neglectful, wealthy Arab mothers. Their humanity is not considered. These migrant workers are largely invisible to many Arabs, and, although there are many exceptions, all too often they are not even considered when it comes to the key ideas of this book, such as generosity, the source of wealth, and friendship. Their stories and perspectives need to be told, but that will have to wait for another book.[6]

I aim to derive practical wisdom for people serving in the Middle East and beyond by understanding the worldview of Middle Easterners regarding righteousness and riches in light of the Bible. No one, to my knowledge, has conducted a comparable study, and I present this work, not as the final word, but as an invitation to fuller discussion.

---

[6] For first-hand accounts of domestic workers living as witnesses to Christ in the Arabian Peninsula, see Adeney, Miriam and Sadiri Joy Tira, *Wealth, Women and God* (Manila, Lifechange, 2014). For a scholarly study of the attitudes of Lebanese Christians to migrant workers and their needs, see Hamd, R. (2012). *Migrant Domestic Workers, The Church, and Mission.* (Doctoral dissertation). Ann Arbor: ProQuest.

1

The Righteous Rich in the Old Testament

Abraham: Our Rich, Righteous Father

We do not know what Abraham's social status was when he received his original call from God, except that he was a freeman and able to support a wife.[7] However, on the way to the fulfillment of that calling, Abraham made an extended stop in Haran, which proved financially lucrative.[8] Neither famine nor a diplomatically disastrous visit to Egypt was able to erode Abraham's acquisitions.[9] On the contrary, we are told that he became very wealthy in livestock and precious metals.[10] So great had become the wealth of Abraham and his nephew that the area in which they were living could not sustain them both and they were forced to separate. So great had become the wealth of Abraham that when his nephew's person and possessions were carried off as booty by the four kings, Abraham had at his disposal his personal army of 318 trained men who were able with the help of the neighbors to defeat the kings' combined forces and come away with Lot, his people and possessions, the rescued population of Sodom, and substantial booty.[11] Although Abraham chose not to profit by this military venture,[12] he did very well out of another diplomatic

---

[7] Genesis 11:29,30. As the story unfolds, it becomes clear that Abraham also had a sense of responsibility for his nephew Lot who traveled with them (Gen 11:31).
[8] Genesis 12:5.
[9] Genesis 12:10—13:1.
[10] Genesis 13:2.
[11] Genesis 14:11–17, 21–24.
[12] Genesis 14:22,23.

disaster, this time with Abimelech, king of Gerar.[13] Shortly before his death, Abraham's servant was able to boast of his master's wealth to Abraham's Mesopotamian relatives,[14] who were doubtless impressed with the servant's 10-camel caravan,[15] the weighty nose ring and bracelets for Rebecca,[16] and the lavish gifts they were given.[17] There is no doubt that Abraham was rich.

He was also righteous. Although there is much in the Genesis account that can be construed as evidence of his righteousness, at one point only is this righteousness explicitly established in the narrative of his journeying with God, and that is at the point of faith: "Abram believed God and it was credited to him as righteousness."[18] It is noteworthy that this faith, though it clearly had underpinnings in specific beliefs about God, was more than acquiescence to correct ideas about God. The object of his faith was God himself and the occasion of his faith was God's promise.

The moment of decisive faith came when God challenged Abram to trust God with his deepest pain and hope, his longing for a son. The profundity of this issue for Abram is evident in his abrupt dismissal of God's promise of reward: "O Sovereign Lord, what can you give me since I remain childless and the one who will inherit my estate is Eliezer of Damascus?"[19] The would-be patriarch valued a son more than all the wealth God could promise, and without the son, the wealth was as much a source of sorrow as of pleasure. When Abraham believed God's promise of a host of descendants, God reiterated his promise of land and made a covenant with Abraham.[20] This combination of faith and covenant laid the foundation for all that follows it in Scripture. The righteousness of Abraham was a righteousness of faith, as Paul forcefully argues in his epistle to the Romans.[21]

---

[13] Genesis 20, and especially verses 14–16.
[14] Genesis 24:34,35.
[15] Genesis 24:10.
[16] Genesis 24:22.
[17] Genesis 24:53.
[18] Genesis 15:5,6.
[19] Genesis 15:1,2. Although the concept that God Himself is one's reward or portion can be found in the Psalms, the response of Abram makes clear that *he* at least understood the last phrase of 15:1 to be a promise of material possessions which could be bequeathed.
[20] Genesis 15:4–21.
[21] Chapter 4.

Nevertheless, James is quick to point out that Abraham's faith was faith that mattered because Abraham acted upon it.[22] This assertion comes in the context of an accusation that someone who does not care for the physical needs of the indigent brother cannot possibly have saving faith.[23] Interestingly, rich Abraham is not held up as an example for someone who fed the poor (Genesis makes no mention of Abraham doing such a thing), but as someone who was willing to make an offering of his greatest treasure, namely his son, because of his faith. James seems to be telling his readers that true faith results in a righteousness that is evident through its willingness to make costly sacrifices. For James' readers, that meant a change of behavior with regard to the poor, whereas for Abraham, it meant binding precious Isaac to the altar.

James connects Abraham's righteousness with the friendship that existed between Abraham and God, and certainly this comes out in the Genesis narrative of Abraham's life.[24] It was on the basis of Abraham's faith that God reckoned Abraham righteous and bound himself to Abraham with a ceremonial oath, an everlasting covenant. Here the relational element of righteousness is at its clearest.

The narrative of Abraham in Genesis, like all biblical narratives, poses difficulties for the Christian ethicist because there is no clear distinction made between what in Abraham's life is to be emulated and what is merely historically descriptive. The Bible portrays nearly all of its great people as flawed and fully human, and Abraham is no exception. And yet he is given this crucial and lengthy role in the narrative because he is indeed a father of many, and children are expected to strive to be like their fathers. Can any more be said of Abraham as a model of the righteous rich beyond his faith which revealed itself in his willingness to sacrifice what he cherished most?

While the narrative's lack of explicit evaluation limits what we can say with certainty, there is no doubt that Abraham displays a

---

[22] James 2:17–24.
[23] James 2:14–16.
[24] For instance, Genesis 17:1.

variety of admirable characteristics associated with righteousness in the Scriptures.[25]

The narrative makes it clear that God had made Abraham rich, in part because of his righteous responses to divine initiative, and that prosperity was included in the blessing God promised to him. If we had only the narrative of Abraham to go by, we might be entitled to think that anyone righteous can expect to prosper. But our next ancient example of the righteous rich would be the first to disabuse us of such a notion.

Job: Permanently Righteous, Temporarily Rich

Abraham and Job had much in common. Like Abraham, Job was a man of the patriarchal period famous for wealth and piety, and highly respected by leading personalities in his region. In both cases, the righteousness of the man was established outside the framework of the Mosaic covenant. Like Abraham, Job was tested, but unlike Abraham's testing, Job's was not entered into voluntarily. Although in very different ways and expressing very different personalities, both Job and Abraham passed the test. Most importantly, both had transforming, personal experiences with God in which they learned something of God's character.

The very first verse of the book of Job establishes his virtue: Job was "blameless and upright; he feared God and shunned evil." In Job, righteousness equals character demonstrated in deeds. In this play of great antiquity, the narrator entertains no doubts about Job's integrity. God himself is impressed.[26] He is proud of Job, and even the Accuser is reduced to impugning motives for want of a genuine flaw with which to indict the man.[27] No one is more convinced of

---

[25] Abraham practiced hospitality (Gen 18:1–8), was generous to his relations (Gen 13:8; 24:22,53), rescued his oppressed nephew at great risk to himself (Gen 14), interceded on behalf of others (Gen 18:16–33), gained respect from neighboring groups and maintained good relations (Gen 23:3–6), earned the devotion of his servant (Gen 24:12), shunned entanglement with evil (Gen 14:22,23), would not credit a human being with what God had done (Gen 14:22,23), tithed to Melchizedek, priest of God Most High (Gen 14:20), consistently obeyed God (Gen 12:1–4; 15:9–10; 17:10,11, 23–27; 22:1–11), worshiped God and offered animal sacrifices (Gen12:7; 13:4; 15:10,11), exercised spiritual influence on his household (Gen 17:23,27), and raised Isaac to fear God and shun compromising attachments (Gen 21:4, 8–14; 22:1–18; 24:1–4). In addition, both Stephen and the author to the Hebrews find merit in the fact that Abraham, for all his wealth, was not a landowner, except for the burial ground he purchased when Sarah died (Acts 7:5,16 and Heb 11:9,10,13–16).
[26] Job 1:8; 2:3.
[27] Job 1:9–11; 2:4.

Job's righteousness than himself, and his protests to his own goodness are loud and long.[28]

The friends of Job, however, remain unconvinced until the very end of the story, when they are forced to rely on the intercessions of righteous Job to atone for their maligning of his virtue.[29] Job's accusing companions insist that he must have done great wickedness while he was still rich, wickedness which resulted in his downfall. They accuse him of having committed the typical sins of the rich: exploitation and callousness toward the poor.[30] Job contradicts this allegation vehemently in his final speech. His self-defense provides us with a vivid portrait of the righteous rich person as understood by Job. Stated in the negative, a rich person of high moral character does NOT:

- allow himself to lust,[31]
- speak falsely or deceive,[32]
- depart from the straight path in lifestyle, attitude, or actions,[33]
- allow himself even to consider adultery,[34]
- deny justice to servants of either gender who have a grievance against him,[35]
- refuse the needs of the poor,[36]
- keep his food to himself (on the contrary, he feeds the poor as family),[37]
- ignore clothing needs of the destitute,[38]
- take advantage of the fatherless, knowing that his influence in the court would enable him to get away with it,[39]
- consider that his security is in his riches,[40]
- revel in his wealth or his ability to amass it,[41]

---

[28] For a few of many examples: Job 9:21; 23:7; 27:6; 31:6; 32:1.
[29] Job 42:7–10. It seems, however, they needed Job's intercession for maligning God rather than Job.
[30] Job 22:6–9. Note similar insinuations by Zophar in Job 20:10 and by Elihu in Job 34:26–29; 36:18–20.
[31] Job 31:1.
[32] Job 31:5. The reference to honest scales in verse 6 may suggest that Job has in mind deceit in business.
[33] Job 31:7. See also Job 23:11,12.
[34] Job 31:9.
[35] Job 31:13.
[36] Job 31:16.
[37] Job 31:17,18.
[38] Job 31:19,20.
[39] Job 31:21.
[40] Job 31:24.
[41] Job 31:25. John E Hartley, *The Book of Job*, (Grand Rapids, Eerdmans, 1988).

- indulge in secret animistic worship,[42]
- gloat over an enemy's troubles,[43]
- curse an enemy,[44]
- withhold hospitality of generous meals and lodging,[45]
- conceal his sins for fear of the crowd's contempt,[46] or
- exploit tenant laborers.[47]

Several things need to be noted about the above list. It is a portrayal, not a code of law.[48] The goodness Job believes God expects of him goes far beyond what any civil legislation could detail, including such qualities as purity of mind and generosity. Yet the blamelessness which Job claims for himself is not sinless perfection.[49]

Job explains the logic of most of his standards solely on the basis of his theology: no merely pragmatic justification is given. For example, both delight in riches and animism are abhorred because they represent infidelity to God,[50] and injustice towards one's servants cannot be countenanced because both the rich man and the servants are fellow creatures of one Creator.[51] The fear of God features prominently in his reasoning. Severe self-imprecations are attached throughout for any moral failure on Job's part, curses carefully chosen to "make the punishment fit the crime."[52] Many of the items on the list are temptations particular to the rich, and their recital as a whole demonstrates Job's awareness that his wealth subjected him to surplus temptations and responsibilities in comparison with others. Job guards himself against wrong-doing both in the acquisition and in the disposition of his wealth.

The sin Job most fears, however, is that either he or his children might sin with their lips and curse God. His sterling response of

---

[42] Job 31:26,27.
[43] Job 31:29.
[44] Job 31:30.
[45] Job 31:31,32.
[46] Job 31:33,34.
[47] Job 31:38,39.
[48] Francis I. Andersen, *Job: Introduction and Commentary* (London, IVP, 1976) and Douglas Stuart, *Old Testament Exegesis: A Primer for Students and Pastors*, 2nd ed. (Philadelphia, Westminster, 1980).
[49] Job 14:17,18; 31:13,33.
[50] Job 31:25-28.
[51] Job 31:13-15.
[52] Chapter 31 of Job is a rather more sober version of W.S. Gilbert's famous song from *The Mikado*, except that Job recommends the particularly fitting cruelties be applied to himself if he has failed, and not to others.

blessing God in the face of overwhelming loss marks him out as truly great in the eyes of God and the narrator.[53] Ironically, in his speeches, Job accuses God of a great deal, including injustice,[54] and this provokes God's angry response,[55] which in turn provokes Job's repentance for what he has said about God.[56] However, there is something about the way that Job, even while accusing God, looks to him for salvation, wisdom, and vindication that makes it plain that Job refuses to give up his hope in God. In a sense his willingness to express his frustration is an expression of his integrity.[57] God never accuses Job of a lack of integrity, but of underestimating the strength and wisdom of the Almighty, and so speaking without knowledge.[58]

If the first verse of the book of Job establishes his blamelessness, the second and third verses establish his wealth in children, livestock, and servants. The book as a whole makes clear that Job treasured the intangibles of the nearness of God, integrity, and wisdom above the tangibles of life.[59] Among the tangibles, children are treasured above wealth.[60] The narrator begins and ends his narrative with Job's children.[61] One of the outstanding features of Job's religious practice was the offering of purifying sacrifices on behalf of his adult children following every party they threw lest their indulgence had caused them to sin.[62] Bildad makes the hurtful accusation that Job's children died for their own wickedness.[63] He further contends that the Lord's punishment of Job for his wickedness entails obliterating his offspring and therefore his memory.[64] God vindicated Job by giving him a new family of seven sons, and three beautiful daughters who would inherit his wealth along with their brothers, and by allowing

---

[53] Job 1:2–2:4; 2:9,10, and 42:7.
[54] Job 6:29; 19:6; 27:2; 34:5.
[55] Job 38:2; 40:1,8.
[56] Job 40:3,4; 41:3.
[57] Job 27:1–5.
[58] Job 38:1,2.
[59] Integrity—Job 1:1–3; 2:9,10; 6:10, 29; 27:5,6. Wisdom—Job 28. The nearness of God—Job 13:15; 29:4–6.
[60] Notice how Job ranks his losses in 29:4–6 and the losses of the wicked in 27:13–19.
[61] Job 1:2; 42:12–16.
[62] Job 1:4,5.
[63] Job 8:4. Whether the speeches of Job are meant simply as philosophical literature or they represent historical conversations, it is hard to imagine the callousness of making such a statement to a man who has lost 10 children in one day. Miserable comforters, indeed!
[64] Job 18:17–19.

him to see the fourth generation of his descendants.⁶⁵ The ultimate position of this vindication hints that this is, in the narrator's eyes, the ultimate wealth this side of the grave.

A great deal is assumed in the book of Job about the social structure of the world in which Job lived and the role of the rich within that structure. When these assumptions are combined, a consistent pattern emerges. Although Job is never given any title, he is a leader⁶⁶—at least he is while he is rich. His leadership gains its authority by virtue of his wealth and his willingness to use that wealth for the benefit of others, who in return bless him, befriend him, and show him honor. Unlike some wealthy people, who use their power to exploit, do violence, and pervert justice, Job is a model of one who could be counted on to show benevolence and to intercede for others before God and the powerful of the earth. He boasts of his role as a revered patron of society this way:⁶⁷

> Oh, for the days when I was in my prime,
> when God's intimate friendship blessed my house,
> when the Almighty was still with me
> and my children were around me,
> when my path was drenched with cream
> and the rock poured out for me streams of olive oil.
>
> When I went to the gate of the city
> and took my seat in the public square,
> the young men saw me and stepped aside
> and the old men rose to their feet;
> the chief men refrained from speaking
> and covered their mouths with their hands;
> the voices of the nobles were hushed,
> and their tongues stuck to the roof of their mouths.

---

⁶⁵ Job 42:13–16.
⁶⁶ Job 29:7–10, 21–25.
⁶⁷ The following lengthy quotations are given in full because of the strong resemblance they bear to the patronage patterns of Middle Eastern society which will be discussed later in the book.

Whoever heard me spoke well of me,
and those who saw me commended me,
because I rescued the poor who cried for help,
and the fatherless who had none to assist him.
The man who was dying blessed me;
I made the widow's heart sing.
I put on righteousness as my clothing;
justice was my robe and my turban.
I was eyes to the blind
and feet to the lame.
I was father to the needy;
I took up the case of the stranger.
I broke the fangs of the wicked
and snatched the victims from their teeth.

I thought, "I will die in my own house,
my days as numerous as the grains of sand."[68]

When Job loses his wealth, he loses his friends and standing in both the extended family and the community as well. As Job puts it:

He has stripped me of my honor
And removed the crown from my head.
. . . .
He has alienated my brothers from me;
my acquaintances are completely estranged from me.
My kinsmen have gone away;
my friends have forgotten me.
My guests and my maidservants count me a stranger;
they look upon me as an alien.
I summon my servant, but he does not answer,
though I beg him with my own mouth.
My breath is offensive to my wife;
I am loathsome to my own brothers.

---

[68] Job 29:4–18. For more along the same lines see Job 29:21–25.

> Even the little boys scorn me;
> when I appear, they ridicule me.
> All my intimate friends detest me;
> Those I love have turned against me.[69]

To add insult to all of these injuries, Job had to bear the scorn of all those, even his best friends, who believed that he had precipitated his own downfall by failing in his role as benefactor of the society.[70]

In frustration, Job turns on God and accuses him of failure as a patron. God refuses to hear Job's cry.[71] He raises his powerful hand to destroy Job.[72] Rather than defending Job from evil men, God turns him over to them.[73] Job expresses his longing for a mediator, one who can plead on his behalf before God, as he had pleaded for the defenseless before human rulers.[74] His own suffering has made Job especially sensitive to the helplessness of the poor, and he questions God's apparent disregard for their care and protection.[75]

In the final chapter of Job's story, before God restores Job's wealth, he restores his standing. God appoints Job as mediator with himself on behalf of his three influential friends.[76] After God blesses Job with twice what he had before, his faithless family and friends come again with gifts to make the rich even richer.[77]

The story of Job in the Bible assumes the existence of a system of patronage and privilege for the wealthy, but it does not present this system as the ideal for society. Throughout the book there are hints that the system has serious flaws as a protection for either the poor or the rich, and as a basis for thinking about God. To begin with, the protection and assistance given to the poor and weak is purely voluntary and dependent on the character of the rich and

---

[69] Job 19:9,13–19. The lack of respect shown to Job by his wife may also have to do with the loss of status she has suffered as a result of Job's demise. Despite their false accusations, Eliphaz, Bildad, and Zophar are outstanding among Job's friends and family for sitting with him in the dust and commiserating with him (Job 2:11–13).
[70] Eliphaz states this outright (Job 22:6–9) and Elihu implies it (34:17–19, 23–30).
[71] Job 30:20,24. Contrast Job 31:13,16.
[72] Job 30:21–23. Contrast Job 31:21–23.
[73] Job 16:9–11.
[74] Job 9:32–35; 33:23f. These passages foreshadow the mediation of Christ, who fulfills the human longing that God himself become the advocate of the helpless.
[75] Job 24:1–12.
[76] Job 42:7–9.
[77] Job 42:10–12.

powerful.[78] Nor does the system guarantee the rich the security they crave. When Job's fortunes turn, he discovers bitterly that his beneficiaries do not seek to repay the social and emotional debt he believes they owe him.[79] Both of these problems stem from a root disease in the system: it promotes the giving of loyalty, honor, and gifts based on self-interest. Aside from three loyal friends, all of Job's relatives and associates desert him in his hour of need and reappear bearing gifts when he is again in a position to help or harm them.[80] Satan clearly expects the same sort of fickleness from Job toward his divine patron.[81] Job's wife sees the situation as does Satan, and expects her husband to quit his faith.[82] The Lord does not reject the logic of Satan's argument, only his application of it to the righteous Job.[83] Foundational to the message of the book of Job is a rejection of self-interested worship and ethics.[84]

In addition to the sociological understanding of wealth in the ancient world, Job gives us theological insights about wealth. Wealth comes from God, who determines the prosperity or poverty of all.[85] Even Satan cannot touch a person's fortune without God's consent.[86] God does allow evil people to prosper by evil means, so wealth is not necessarily a sign of piety in a person.[87] God is not answerable to human beings about how he distributes plenty and penury,[88] and he is worthy of praise, regardless of what he sends a person.[89] Finally, the whole of the book of Job revolves around the truth that poverty, even sudden disaster, is not necessarily a sign of anything

---

[78] Job 24:1–12.
[79] Job 30:9,10.
[80] Job 19:13–19; 42:11.
[81] Job 1:9–11; 2:4,5.
[82] Job 2:9,10.
[83] Job 1:8,12; 2:3,6.
[84] Another indication of the failure of the system of patronage in the book is more subtle. Job comes to believe that the honor he enjoyed due to his wealth and his gracious disposal of it was his right. His compassion for the poor does not extend to the point of regarding them with honor (Job 30:1–11). His anger at the treatment he is given in his days of distress is not anger at the injustice of despising the poor in general, but at the injustice of such a wonderful person (in his own estimation) being so abused.
[85] Many passages throughout the book, among them 1:20; 42:10,12.
[86] Job 1:10–12; 2:3.
[87] Job 24:1–14. But Job acknowledges that the evil rich are destroyed in the end (v. 18–24).
[88] Job 40:1–8.
[89] Job 1:20.

blameworthy in the sufferer, and that the poor are in need of friends to sit with them in the dust offering comfort without condemnation.

Deuteronomy

Righteousness in Deuteronomy
With the giving of the Law of Moses, a new dimension was added to the biblical concept of righteousness. Moses encouraged the tribes of Israel at the close of his days with this assurance: "And if we are careful to obey all this law before the LORD our God, as he has commanded us, that will be our righteousness."[90] The formation of the people of Israel as a righteous nation depended, of necessity, upon obedience to the law of God as a whole people. Not only were God and people described as righteous, but the injunctions of the Law were "righteous" in that they were just and promoted faithfulness toward the covenant.[91]

Nevertheless, as James Dunn points out,[92] the Law was never intended to be a substitute for relationship. The Law was only given after the relationship was established; a relationship based on God's faithfulness to his covenant promises displayed in his saving acts. The jewel of the Law maintains its value only as it remains in its divinely chosen setting of love.[93] Although human love for God is essential to the fulfillment of the Law, God's love came first and formed the basis of the keeping of the Law.[94]

Moses was very aware as he reiterated the Law to the people in Deuteronomy that they were people who lived in families.[95] The relationship God had with the people had been initiated with their forefathers,[96] and the land which they were going to possess had been promised to their ancestors[97] and, thus, was to be possessed as an

---
[90] Deuteronomy 6:25.
[91] Deuteronomy 4:8.
[92] James D. G. Dunn and Alan M Suggate. *The Justice of God: A Fresh Look at the Old Doctrine of Justification by Faith* (Grand Rapids, Eerdmans, 1993), p. 34. Dunn makes this comment with direct reference to Deuteronomy 5:1–29:1.
[93] Deuteronomy 6:5,6; 10:12,13.
[94] Deuteronomy 10:15,16; 4:37–40; 7:8–11; 33:3,4.
[95] The significance of this paragraph for the project will become clear in the discussions of wealth and relationships later in the book.
[96] Deuteronomy 4:31.
[97] Deuteronomy 26:15 and many other passages.

inheritance.[98] God's punishment of those who hated him extended to the children and their children,[99] but his blessings on the faithful were to be passed down from generation to generation as well.[100] Therefore, what God revealed to the people belongs not only to them, but also to their children.[101] Children were to be included in the rituals and celebrations of the covenant.[102] True righteousness must be taught diligently to the next generation, not by rote learning of the Law only, but by discussion of its application in all aspects of daily life.[103]

Wealth in Deuteronomy

Moses was no Platonist. As one reads through the book of Deuteronomy, one cannot escape the message that prosperity is a blessing which comes from God. It is a sign of his love, and a reward to those who obey him. On numerous occasions through the book, Moses reminds the people in great detail of the material benefits they and their children will enjoy if they are faithful in keeping the Law with their whole hearts.[104] The loss of all sorts of material prosperity is detailed among the curses upon those who do not keep the Law.[105] Ideally, there were to be no poor among God's people because of his generosity and theirs.[106] The basic understanding of wealth in Deuteronomy is that it is good and given by God to people faithful to him.

But it's not that simple. A great many qualifying statements must be added to this foundational assertion if it is accurately to reflect the perspective of Deuteronomy on wealth. To begin with, throughout the book prosperity is part of a larger package of well-being which

---

[98] The idea of inheritance is repeated continually. A few examples are Deuteronomy 2:31; 4:21,38; 12:9; 15:4; 16:20; 19:10; 21:23.
[99] Deuteronomy 5:9 and 29:22. However, God reserves this vengeance on the children for himself. The Law is clear that human authorities must not punish children for their parents' offenses or vice versa (24:16). Deuteronomy 28:53–58 is a particularly gruesome example of God's vengeance affecting the next generation.
[100] Deuteronomy 5:10; 5:16; 12:25, 28; 30:2,6,19,20.
[101] Deuteronomy 29:29.
[102] Deuteronomy 12:4–7.
[103] Deuteronomy 6:6–9; 4:9,10; 11:19–21.
[104] The blessings of Deuteronomy 28:1–13 provide a concentrated example. Zebulon and Issachar are given a blessing of wealth, and Gad is even commended for taking the best land for himself (Deuteronomy 33:18–21). Note the connections with righteousness in this passage.
[105] The curses of Deuteronomy 28:14–68.
[106] Deuteronomy 15:1–11.

includes health, fertile land, favorable weather, financial liquidity and surplus, political and military superiority, honor, holiness, prolific livestock, abundant food, and many children.[107] The gaining of money by itself for its own sake is never contemplated. The amassing of gold and silver is forbidden.[108] The issue, as Moses puts it, is "life and prosperity."[109] God himself has chosen the people for his own treasured inheritance,[110] and the inheritance of the Levites is God himself[111] in lieu of a tribal allotment. The possession of Jacob was not only the land, but also the Law.[112]

Second, the wealth that is described in such appealing detail in Deuteronomy is not opulent or excessive. The speeches of Deuteronomy are addressed to extremely poor people who are about to enjoy sufficiency and surplus for the first time in 400 years.[113] The prosperity described in the book should be viewed in that light. The list of things God blesses includes such simple and essential items as the family basket and kneading bowl.[114] Extravagant luxury is strictly forbidden, even for God's choice of a king.[115] If there were to be no poor among the people, neither were there to be any extremely rich.[116]

Third, all wealth is from God.[117] God never tires in Deuteronomy of telling the people that he is the one giving them the land "flowing with milk and honey,"[118] and all of its blessings.[119] He is the owner of all there is,[120] and therefore has the right to give commands about how it should be used. It is God who gives the ability to produce wealth,

---

[107] Deuteronomy 33:22–28.
[108] Deuteronomy 17:17.
[109] Deuteronomy 30:15.
[110] Deuteronomy 9:26,29; 26:18,19; 32:9. According to the last of these passages, the holiness (in the sense of being set apart) of the people is a direct result of God's declaration that they are his treasured inheritance.
[111] Deuteronomy 18:2.
[112] Deuteronomy 33:4.
[113] Consider Deuteronomy 12:20, where Moses mentions as a luxury a diet which includes meat.
[114] Deuteronomy 28:5.
[115] Deuteronomy 17:14–20. 1 Kings 10:26–28 demonstrates how exactly and thoroughly King Solomon violated the Law.
[116] Deuteronomy 15:4. This ideal quickly gives way to reality in v. 11. Perhaps the ideal expressed in 17:14–20 is equally unrealistic.
[117] Deuteronomy 8:6–9.
[118] Deuteronomy 6:3.
[119] Deuteronomy 4:1,21,38; 5:30; 11:14,15,31; 17:14; 18:9; 19:1; 20:16; 21:23; 24:4; 27:3; 28:8.
[120] Deuteronomy 10:14.

so boasting of one's ability to produce wealth is unacceptable.[121] He gives to whom he chooses, and he takes back what he has given.[122] Although private ownership is assumed throughout the book, that ownership is never seen as absolute, but subject to God's right to bless and withhold.

Fourth, in Deuteronomy, the gifts of God are not given based on human righteousness, but their retention is dependent upon keeping the Law.[123] Moses takes pain in 9:4–6 to make the people understand that their acquisition of the land has nothing whatsoever to do with their righteousness or integrity. Rather, the wickedness of the nations explains why God has determined to give the land to the tribes of Israel. If Israel behaves as did the previous nations in the land God cares for,[124] they will also be destroyed for lack of obedience.[125] While God is the ultimate dispenser of fortune and woe, he nevertheless allows people to make informed choices which have real consequences for all of life, including economic well-being.[126] With the giving of the land came the giving of the Law.

A fifth qualification of the positive attitude toward wealth expressed in Deuteronomy is the clear and repeated warning that wealth is dangerous. The very blessing which came from God may cause his people to become proud and forget him.[127] God intended the tribes of Israel to take this great danger very seriously, and he predicted through Moses his prophet that they would fall into the forgetfulness brought about by wealth, and be devastated. This is the theme of the song which Moses taught to the people as a witness against them.[128]

Sixth, the appropriate responses to divine generosity are praise, remembering God, and joyful obedience to his commands.[129] In particular, the book of Deuteronomy is full of reminders not to

---

[121] Deuteronomy 8:17,18.
[122] Deuteronomy 2:20–23 is one example, an example which should not be neglected in thinking theologically about the Israeli/Palestinian conflict.
[123] Deuteronomy 4:25; 27:3.
[124] Deuteronomy 11:12.
[125] Deuteronomy 8:19,20.
[126] Deuteronomy 30:15–20.
[127] Deuteronomy 6:10–12; 8:12–18; 31:20; 32:13–15.
[128] Deuteronomy 31:21. The song comprises most of chapter 32.
[129] Moses rebukes the people for their failure to respond suitably in Deuteronomy 8:10,11; 28:47.

forget. They were to remember his saving acts and his greatness.[130] They were not to forget that God was their Father, that he owed them nothing,[131] and that they owed him their very existence.[132]

A seventh qualification to the positive portrayal of wealth in Deuteronomy is that poverty teaches wealthy people how to use their wealth. The people were reminded of their experience of slavery in Egypt as a basis for empathy with the poor and obedience to laws protecting the vulnerable.[133] The writer of Deuteronomy sensed the very real danger that the social distance created by the wealth of some would lead to tightfistedness, ruthless financial dealings, and lack of mercy. The Law, in Deuteronomy and elsewhere, is concerned with attitude as well as action. Even the king himself is to remember that he is no better than his fellow Israelites, and equally under the Law.[134]

Finally, although the giving of an abundant land was an expression of God's love,[135] so too was the great hardship they had experienced in forty years of desert wanderings.[136]

Wealth and the Commands

What follows is *not* a detailed analysis of the whole of the Deuteronomic legal system in light of the theme of the righteous rich, but a humble attempt to point out a few particularly salient injunctions. Passages have been selected on the basis of their relevance to the key themes about the righteous rich in the Scriptures in general or Deuteronomy in particular, or on the basis of the relevance to significant findings about the concept of the righteous rich in Middle Eastern societies.

---

[130] Deuteronomy 4:7,9.
[131] Deuteronomy 9:4–24.
[132] Deuteronomy 32:18.
[133] Deuteronomy 5:12–15; 10:17–22; 15:12–18; 16:11,12; 24:17–22.
[134] Deuteronomy 17:19,20.
[135] Deuteronomy 4:37,38.
[136] Deuteronomy 8:2–5.

They are given in the order in which they appear in Deuteronomy.
- Moses enjoins officials to judge impartially, whether the case involves great or small, Israelite or alien. They are not to fear anyone but God.[137]
- The Sabbath is a clear statement of the priority God must be given over the means of wealth, and of the fact that humans were made for something other than merely work. Getting others to do one's work on the Sabbath is also forbidden. Slaves, aliens, and even animals need time to rest and honor God.[138]
- The command to honor parents carries with it a promise of general well-being in the land.[139]
- Both theft and covetousness are prohibited.[140] The latter of these could never be enforced in a court of law, but it is as fully part of the Ten Commandments as the other nine. Coveting the gold and silver of the idols of the inhabitants of the land was a sin particularly to be avoided.[141] So was the plunder from an advocate of idolatry.[142]
- Israel's wealth was to be gained at a horrible price: the total destruction of other nations.[143] This was a specific act of God for a specific time. As we shall see below, within Israel itself, it was forbidden to build one's fortune ruthlessly on the demise of others, and the economic devastation of an Israelite person or family was never to be considered permanent.
- Acceptable worship was financially costly, involving "burnt offerings and sacrifices, your tithes, and special gifts."[144]
- Levites were to benefit from the tithes of others,[145] suggesting that ministers should receive financial remuneration.

---

[137] Deuteronomy 1:16,17. In fact, the Law itself allows a great deal of discrimination against non-Israelites, for instance, in matters of debt cancellation (15:3), usury (23:19–20), release from slavery (15:12), and participation in worship (23:1–7). But a basic principle of impartiality is established at the beginning of the book.
[138] Deuteronomy 5:12–15.
[139] Deuteronomy 5:16. Furthermore, Jesus interprets this command in terms of the financial obligations children bear toward their parents.
[140] Deuteronomy 5:19,21.
[141] Deuteronomy 7:25.
[142] Deuteronomy 13:16,17.
[143] Deuteronomy 7.
[144] Deuteronomy 12:6; 27:7.
[145] Deuteronomy 12:18; 14:27–29; 18:1–8.

- The special tithe at the end of three years was to be shared with the Levite, alien, fatherless, and widow.[146] God's blessing was conditional upon sharing in proportion to one's wealth.[147]
- All debts of fellow Israelites were to be canceled unconditionally every seven years.[148]
- Hard heartedness toward the poor was a sin. It was wrong to avoid making a loan to a poor person because one might not be able to collect on it. Generous and ungrudging giving was commanded.[149]
- Israelite slaves were to be manumitted every seven years and given the supplies necessary to succeed as freed people. Owners of slaves were not to view their release as a hardship.[150]
- God always got the firstborn animals.[151] This was an ongoing reminder of God's ultimate ownership.
- Children, Levites, and the vulnerable were all to be included in the celebration of the Feast of Weeks.[152]
- Everyone was required to bring something as an offering at the three Feasts of Unleavened Bread, Weeks, and Tabernacles, proportional to the blessing they had received from God.[153] No one was excused from bringing an offering.
- It was forbidden for judges to accept bribes, "for a bribe blinds the eyes of the wise and twists the words of the righteous."[154]
- Assistance had to be given to a neighbor who had lost property.[155]
- Slaves in search of refuge were to be assisted and not returned to their masters.[156]
- The earnings of a prostitute were not acceptable as offerings to God.[157]
- No Israelite could be charged interest on a loan.[158]

---

[146] Deuteronomy 14:28,29.
[147] Compare 1 Corinthians 16:2.
[148] Deuteronomy 15:1–3.
[149] Deuteronomy 15:7–11.
[150] Deuteronomy 15:12–18.
[151] Deuteronomy 15:19.
[152] Deuteronomy 16:11,12.
[153] Deuteronomy 16:16,17.
[154] Deuteronomy 16:19; 27:25.
[155] Deuteronomy 22:1–4.
[156] Deuteronomy 23:15,16
[157] Deuteronomy 23:17,18.
[158] Deuteronomy 23:19.

- It was against God's Law to keep as collateral for a loan something essential to the person's livelihood or health.[159] God regarded it as a righteous act to return by nightfall a cloak taken in pledge.
- Poor workers were to be paid daily by sunset.[160]
- Owners of agricultural land were not to harvest thoroughly, but to leave produce behind in the fields for the destitute.[161]
- Cheating in measurement (differing weights) was hateful to God and therefore banned.[162]
- The boundaries of family land were to remain inviolate.[163]

In this hodgepodge of legislation, certain principles recur. The overarching emphasis in the Law is that the wealthy must think and act justly (righteously) and that the poor are to be protected, helped, and treated with dignity. Would the warnings of Deuteronomy be sufficient to guard the people against the dangers of the wealth with which God would bless them? Moses knew they would not. Next we will consider the epitome of a person whose God-given wealth was used to showcase his success, but led to his failure.

Solomon

Solomon was born into a wealthy, powerful family, but he far exceeded his father's economic and political greatness, building on the spiritual, military, political, and financial successes of King David. David's rise to power is attributed in the Bible to the favor of God and to David's righteousness.[164] Solomon's greater ascendancy is attributed to his God-given wisdom.

In the Old Testament, wisdom is the practical art of being successful.[165] This success is viewed, not with a capitalist "bottom line" mentality, but with a Semitic holism which recognizes that success in one arena of life without success in another is a stunted success at best. To put it in contemporary terms, the wise person of

---

[159] Deuteronomy 24:6,10–13,17,18.
[160] Deuteronomy 24:14,15.
[161] Deuteronomy 24:19–22.
[162] Deuteronomy 25:13–16.
[163] Deuteronomy 27:17.
[164] 1 Kings 3:6.
[165] Douglas, J. D. *et al*, *The Illustrated Bible Dictionary*, Vol. 3 (Leicester: IVP, 1980), p. 1650.

the Bible would score high in an evaluation of a variety of types of intelligence: spiritual, moral, social, economic, emotional, academic, and so on. The most foundational of these types of intelligence is "the fear of the LORD,"[166] a wholesome respect for God's character and power that leads to moral prudence. Solomon started with this essential foundation of godly fear, and God supplied the wisdom which ensured Solomon political domination,[167] diplomatic finesse,[168] extreme economic prosperity,[169] administrative savvy,[170] judicial prudence,[171] competence in civil engineering and architecture,[172] vast general knowledge,[173] and liturgical leadership.[174]

It would be hard to overstate the wealth of Solomon.[175] His was an absolute monarchy, and no distinction was made between the national treasury and the king's personal wealth.[176] His affluence was internationally famous, and the Queen of Sheba was overwhelmed when she saw it in person.[177]

Solomon had enough wisdom and character to ensure that others also benefited by it. There was a general economic upsurge during his reign, particularly in Jerusalem.[178] The king greatly enhanced national pride and made lasting contributions to the public life and security of the nation through his massive building projects.[179] He was capable of dispensing lavish gifts.[180] Most enduringly, he built

---

[166] Proverbs 1:7.
[167] 1 Kings 4:1,21,24–25.
[168] 1 Kings 4:34; 10:1–13.
[169] 1 Kings 9:26–28; 10:14–29.
[170] 1 Kings 4: 27,28, 9:19–24, 26–28.
[171] 1 Kings 3:16–28; 10:8,9.
[172] 1 Kings 6:1–7:12.
[173] 1 Kings 4:29–34.
[174] 1 Kings 8:1–66; 9:25.
[175] 2 Chronicles 9:13–28 is one of several descriptions in the Bible of Solomon's wealth. In addition to the passages in 1 Kings and 2 Chronicles which enthuse about the extravagant splendor of Solomon's lifestyle and property, there are hints of the same in the Song of Solomon and in Ecclesiastes.
[176] For example, the tribute received from vassal states, 500 shields, the gifts brought by visiting dignitaries, the thousands of horses and hundreds of chariots of the Israelite army—all of these are described as Solomon's (2 Chronicles 9:13–28). He was able to maintain 300 wives of royal birth and 700 concubines, and he built an elaborate palace for one of his wives, the daughter of Pharaoh (1 Kings 11:1–3; 7:8). The king owned 1,400 imported chariots and 12,000 imported horses (2 Chronicles 1:14–17).
[177] 2 Chronicles 9:4.
[178] 1 Kings 4:20, 25; 2 Chronicles 1:14–17; 9:20, 27.
[179] 1 Kings 9:15–18, 27; 4:25.
[180] 2 Chronicles 9:12. However, Hiram felt insulted by the quality of the 10 cities that Solomon gave him in recognition of Hiram's huge contribution to Israel's public building projects and navy, and this lack of generosity on Solomon's part soured a fine relationship of long standing.

a magnificent temple in Jerusalem to Yahweh where he presented abundant sacrifices.[181]

The Bible has a great deal to say about the vast wealth and exemplary wisdom of Solomon, but little about his righteousness. Only the Queen of Sheba, on what was obviously a diplomatic, relationship-enhancing trip, spoke confidently about Solomon's ability to "maintain justice and righteousness," particularly in the context of handing down wise decisions in legal matters.[182] In this aspect of righteousness, the Bible is in complete agreement with the Queen: Solomon was a master of insightful jurisprudence.[183] But neither the narrators nor God himself ever declare Solomon righteous. This is not to claim he had no good qualities—on the contrary. In addition to those already named, Solomon exhibited a degree of humility unusual in a man of his ability, and he was careful to give God the credit for his impressive achievements, particularly early in his reign. But, "as Solomon grew old, his wives turned his heart after other gods, and his heart was not fully devoted to the LORD his God, as the heart of David his father had been. . . . he (Solomon) did not follow the LORD completely, as David his father had done."[184]

Despite King Solomon's blatant disregard for the stern injunctions of Deuteronomy 17, neither the author of 1 Kings nor that of 2 Chronicles speaks a word against his ostentatious wealth.[185] However, in 1 Kings[186] the blame for Solomon's spiritual demise is intimately related to his fortune and elevated position. Solomon could afford to indulge his love of foreign women,[187] and no doubt this self-indulgence paid off in terms of trade, gifts received, and diplomatic

---

[181] 2 Chronicles 3–5 (although it must be noted that King David had already donated and raised an enormous sum toward the building of the temple as described in 1 Chronicles 29:1–9, and it was his final wish that Solomon build the temple which he himself was forbidden to build); 1 Chronicles 29:21; 2 Chronicles 8:12,13.

[182] 1 Kings 10:9 and its parallel 2 Chronicles 9:8.

[183] 1 Kings 3:11,28.

[184] 1 Kings 11:4,6.

[185] Nor do they censure his exploitation of aliens, contrary to God's law, or his forbidden relationship with Egypt.

[186] As against 2 Chronicles. 2 Chronicles tends to tell only the glorious side of Solomon's reign, while the author of 1 Kings is rather more willing to expose the great king's faults and failures.

[187] 1 Kings 11:1–3.

relations,[188] in addition to personal gratification. As predicted by God, marriage to pagan wives provided a powerful temptation first to tolerate, and then to participate in, idolatrous practices.[189] It would have been no easy task to forbid a large number of influential and homesick princesses, many of whom were permanently excluded from Israel's worship, to abandon completely their religious heritages. The builder of the LORD's temple became also the builder of a number of pagan temples in the region of Jerusalem.[190]

I find it noteworthy that, at this point, no prophet stepped forth to confront Solomon with his great evil, no Nathan or Elijah. One can only speculate why this was so. Solomon financed the building and running of the temple, including providing the daily sacrifices. At the dedication of the temple, he, and not the priest, had uttered the prayer of dedication. He deposed and appointed the priests.[191] He also appointed all of the secular officials, too.[192] He had established his reign by executing a number of people who were potential threats to him.[193] The king also had a large popular following in Judea, and especially around Jerusalem, for many had benefited financially through his building projects, international trade agreements, and royal extravagance. It would have taken a great deal of courage and confidence to confront such a man. Perhaps in Solomon's day, it did not profit to be a prophet.[194] His wealth and power bought for him a kind of immunity from accountability, except before the God who had loaned Solomon all his power and wealth.

Solomon, who had received such a grand heritage of righteousness from his father, frittered it away in his later years. When Rehoboam took the throne, he displayed neither the righteousness of his grandfather David nor the wisdom of his father Solomon. As a result of his first major decision, the kingdom was divided, and by the end of his reign, the great temple Solomon had built was

---

[188] It is no coincidence that 1 Kings 11:1 was connected in the author's mind with the preceding chapter which describes the mutually beneficial visit of the Queen of Sheba and the extent and variety of Solomon's international diplomatic and trade relations.
[189] Exodus 34:16; Deuteronomy 17:17.
[190] 1 Kings 11:7,8.
[191] 1 Kings 2:26,27,35.
[192] 1 Kings 4:4–7.
[193] 1 Kings 2:13–46.
[194] Corny humor thanks to Perry Shaw.

pillaged by the king of Egypt.[195] The pagan practices introduced by Solomon's wives became popularized,[196] which was not surprising considering that Rehoboam's mother was an Ammonite.[197] The four months per year of forced labor which Solomon extracted from his own people (in addition to the enslavement of all aliens except his wives) was clearly resented by the 10 northern tribes which did not share to the same extent as Judah the benefits of Solomon's reign, and this discontent led to division under Rehoboam. For all of his excellent and God-given virtues, Solomon is, nevertheless, a dubious example of the righteous rich.

The Proverbs

If Solomon failed to teach wisdom to his son, Rehoboam, it was not through lack of interest in the subject of teaching wisdom to the next generation. He is famed for his collection of 3000 proverbs,[198] and nearly a third of the canonical collection of wise sayings compiled in his honor is devoted specifically to exhorting sons to learn wisdom. This may well have been the purpose of the collection as a whole. As mentioned above, this wisdom was practical advice which, if followed, would enable the young men to whom they are addressed to achieve success in life.[199] This practical advice is woven firmly around a moral framework which impacts all areas of life. In keeping with our topic of "the righteous rich," the rest of this section seeks to describe the relationship between wealth and righteousness in the Proverbs with special reference to some of the themes which will emerge later in the discussion of perceptions of "the righteous rich" in the Middle East.

---

[195] 1 Kings 14:25,26.
[196] 1 Kings 14:22-24.
[197] 1 Kings 14:21,31.
[198] 1 Kings 4:32.
[199] I will use the term "son" in this section to reflect the male orientation of the proverbs themselves. While much of the wisdom of Proverbs is equally applicable for females, the wording of the book consistently assumes a male audience.

The Proverbs which were collected in Solomon's name and tradition[200] do not have a problem with money *per se*. In the tradition of Solomon, wealth is seen as good and desirable, a source of security,[201] the reward of God, and the result of hard work and wise choices. But the Proverbs do consistently teach that money isn't everything,[202] that it mustn't be obtained at the price of involvement in violence or injustice,[203] that it ought not to be gained quickly or by fraud,[204] that care must be taken to maintain it,[205] and that it should be used—with care—for the good of others and not just self.[206]

Although some of the Proverbs concern the affairs of ordinary people, many others indicate that the intended audience of the collection had access to money and to people in high places. Therefore, the morality expressed in Proverbs bears direct relation to our study of "the righteous rich." What are some of the issues facing the righteous rich according to the Proverbs?

One is the issue of beneficence and patronage. "When the righteous prosper, the city rejoices."[207] The city rejoices not simply because they have a positive attitude toward righteousness in the abstract, but that righteous people, when they succeed, benefit the city, becoming patrons and advocates for justice. They contribute to projects which bring civic pride,[208] and they are generous to the poor.[209] They are able to use their influence to ensure that justice is

---

[200] The book of Proverbs itself ascribes its final two chapters to persons other than Solomon and states clearly that its final compilation did not take place before the days of Hezekiah (Prov 25:1). Nevertheless, the collection makes three ascriptions to Solomon as its source (Prov 1:1, 10:1, and 25:1). Therefore, it seems safe to view this biblical collection of proverbial wisdom as being associated with Solomon in the minds of the compilers, and may well include a number of sayings collected or composed by David's heir. Personally, I agree with F. Delitzsch ("Proverbs, Ecclesiastes, Song of Solomon," vol. VI of *Commentary on the Old Testament in Ten Volumes* by C. F. Keil and F. Delitzsch, trans. James Martin, Grand Rapids: Eerdmans, 1980) that it seems unreasonable to suppose that the redactors managed to edit out every last one of Solomon's proverbs, although "there must always be some uncertainty as to the exact amount of the proverbial literature that may be said to be strictly Solomonic" (Roland Kenneth Harrison, *Introduction to the Old Testament*, Grand Rapids: Eerdmans, 1969, 1014).

[201] Proverbs 10:15.
[202] Proverbs 15:16,17; 16:8; 17:16, 19:1; 25:11,12,24; 28:6.
[203] Proverbs 1:10–19; 4:14–17.
[204] Proverbs 13:11; 20:17.
[205] Proverbs 12:27.
[206] Proverbs 19:17.
[207] Proverbs 11:10.
[208] Note the following verse (11:11). The "blessing" here refers to more than mere words, just as "the mouth of the wicked" refers to more than just the things the wicked say. See also 29:2.
[209] Proverbs 19:17.

done,[210] and to raise the general moral climate.[211] Note the assumption that it is the influence of successful, righteous individuals, as against formal government structures, which is considered the normal means of obtaining civic well-being. Those in powerful positions have a particular responsibility to uphold righteousness.[212] Not only is patronage a sign of righteousness; it is also a sign of wisdom.[213] By using one's influence to benefit others and by giving gifts, for instance, one enhances one's popularity.[214] When people feel they have a trustworthy and loving king, they will love him in return, and the love of the people is the king's security.[215] Therefore, it is better to be generous and receive generosity and goodwill in return, than to hoard one's wealth which is a false security.[216] "A good name is more desirable than great riches; to be esteemed is better than silver or gold."[217] However, the Proverbs do not distinguish between patronage unselfishly done for others, and negative patronage done to "keep people in line" and minimize their opposition. Solomon established a good name in Jerusalem and among those of his own tribe, but failed to win the hearts of the northern tribes, who clearly felt used.[218]

Although many contemporary Westerners would frown on it, the Proverbs advise the use of gifts to the great as a means of gaining access to the rich, although they note some of the problems entailed in giving to them.[219] Six times the Proverbs refer to what Westerners might consider bribes. Three of these instances are clearly negative, but three speak positively about "gifts."[220] Like all proverbs, those of the Bible are not laws to be followed in all situations, but gems of wisdom which only gleam in the correct setting. The righteous rich will shun the giving and receiving of justice-perverting bribes,

---

[210] Proverbs 22:22,23.
[211] Proverbs 20:29; 29:12.
[212] Proverbs 16:10–12; 17:26; 24:10–12; 25:23–25; 31:8,9.
[213] Proverbs 11:30.
[214] Proverbs 19:6.
[215] Proverbs 14:24; 20:28.
[216] Proverbs 11:16,17,24–28.
[217] Proverbs 22:1.
[218] 1 Kings 12:3,4.
[219] Proverbs 18:16 contrasted with 22:16.
[220] The positive references are Proverbs 17:8; 18:16; 21:14. The negative references are 15:27; 17:23; 22:16.

but leave the door open for prudent use of gifts to sooth the anger of others and to extend one's own positive influence.[221] Solomon himself was certainly not averse in practice to the strategic use of gifts, and he both gave and received many.

Another issue addressed by the Proverbs is that of the relationship between rich and poor. A true friend continues to love even in adversity,[222] but what normally happens is that the poor are abandoned while everyone clamors around the rich.[223] It is not wrong to seek prosperity as a result of long-term, sensible hard work, but it is wrong to become proud as well as rich.[224] Although the assumption throughout the Proverbs is that the rich will rule and rulers will be rich,[225] there lingers a certain egalitarianism with regard to respect, since both rich and poor are the product of the same Maker.[226] One should also be alert to the fact that people pretend to be either richer or poorer than they actually are, and some rich people's apparent hospitality is insincere.[227]

How one makes one's money is an important issue for the righteous rich in Proverbs. Bribery, robbery, usury, fraud, violence, and oppression are evil means of gain and will fail to bring lasting blessing.[228] Attempts to get rich quick are both unwise and immoral.[229] How one uses one's money is also important. Self-indulgence is frowned on in the Proverbs, and drinking in excess is particularly inappropriate to the rich.[230] The Proverbs have a great deal to say, and all of it negative, about the dissipation of wealth through idleness. Most importantly, the rich are called on to be generous to the poor.[231]

---

[221] For an excellent consideration of bribery and gifts in cross-cultural ethical dilemmas, see chapter 7, "Ethical Theory and Bribery," in Adeney, Bernard T. *Strange Virtues: Ethics in a Multicultural World.* (Leicester: Apollos, 1995).
[222] Proverbs 17:17.
[223] Proverbs 14:20; 19:4,7.
[224] Proverbs 14:21; 21:4.
[225] Proverbs 22:7 is one example.
[226] Proverbs 17:5; 22:2.
[227] Proverbs 12:9; 13:7; 23:6–8; 25:14.
[228] For example, Proverbs 1:8–19; 22:22–23,28; 28:8,24.
[229] Proverbs 20:21; 23:4,5; 28:20,22.
[230] Proverbs 21:17; 31:4–7.
[231] It is noteworthy that the very frequent and impassioned protests in Proverbs against idleness are directed, not to the poor, but to wealthy young men who stand to be ruined by their sloth. Never in the Proverbs are the injunctions against laziness intended as a justification for tightfistedness toward the needy. On the contrary, the book of Proverbs consistently enjoins respectful, compassionate liberality. A few examples include Proverbs 14:21; 19:17; 22:9.

The great building projects of Solomon, his wealth, and his harem are all gone. However, the wisdom of his tradition remains with us in this collection of adages which readers of the Scriptures have found helpful for righteous and prosperous living over many centuries and across many cultures. Later in this book, echoes of Solomon's life and the Proverbs will resonate from the Middle East in the twenty-first century, as if the land itself had witnessed the wisdom of Solomon and remembered.

The Unrighteous Rich and Amos
One doesn't learn anything at all about the righteous rich from Amos, except by implication. The bulk of the book is a prophecy of woe against the *un*righteous rich of Israel, and God's spokesman doesn't indulge them in flattery. Amos has a great deal to tell us about what the righteous rich are *not*.

To begin with, the righteous rich would not drive the poor into the ground.[232] One of Amos' most devastating complaints against the well-off of the Northern Kingdom was that they sold the poor into slavery to recover paltry sums, no more than the price of a pair of sandals.[233] In contempt of the Law of God, they slept on garments taken from the poor as collateral for a loan.[234] These were people for whom money ranked far above the godly virtues of forgiveness, compassion, mercy, and love. In this they were no better than their neighboring pagan enemies.[235] Their attitude was, "Pay what you owe me now, or you'll pay with your freedom." The desperate state of their debtors was not taken into account, nor was their own considerable affluence.[236] Although the men handled most of the financial matters, the women were also culpable through their greedy encouragement of their husbands.[237]

But it was not simply a matter of the rich callously getting what they were entitled to by law. The unrighteous, rich audience

---
[232] Amos 2:6,7; 3:9; 4:1; 8:6.
[233] Amos 2:6; 8:6.
[234] Amos 2:8.
[235] Compare with the prophecies against Gaza and Tyre in Amos 1.
[236] According to 2 Kings 14:25,27, Israel went through a period of expansion and recovery during the reign of Jeroboam II, despite the fact that he did evil in the eyes of the Lord.
[237] Amos 4:1.

of Amos manipulated the courts to get more than that to which they were entitled. The poor were deprived of justice.[238] Through their connections in court or through bribery, the rich were able to make a practice of extortion and oppression, and there was nothing the poor could do.[239] Those with limited incomes had no recourse when the wealthy cheated them in trade or manipulated the market unfairly.[240] It stands to reason, then, that the righteous rich abstain from unethical business practices, *whether or not these practices are legally sanctioned*. They do not use their influence in court to skirt laws designed to protect the consumer or the poor.

Although Amos tended to focus his condemnation on certain observable behaviors of the rich, it is clear that underlying it all is a concern about attitude. The violent and greedy do not even know how to do right.[241] The complacency of the self-indulgent sickens Amos.[242] Just as Tyre and Edom were condemned for their lack of fellow-feeling or compassion,[243] so Amos throughout seems flabbergasted by the inability of Israel's upper crust to empathize with their poor compatriots, and by their total lack of concern at the damage they are doing to the nation.[244] By implication, the righteous rich consider the effect of their choices on the nation as a whole. They will refuse to profit by the oppression or humiliation of the vulnerable. The righteous rich seek good, hate evil, and maintain justice in courts of law.[245]

Amos is extremely critical of the lifestyles of the rich, which are extravagant, self-indulgent, and built upon oppression.[246] He particularly criticizes the ownership of multiple dwellings, the elaborate interior design of the houses,[247] the beds and couches,[248] the eagerness for drink,[249] and the feasting, lounging, and entertainment

---

[238] Amos 5:7,10,12.
[239] Amos 5:11,12.
[240] Amos 8:5,6.
[241] Amos 3:10.
[242] Amos 6:1,8.
[243] Amos 1:9,11.
[244] Amos 3:9, 6:6.
[245] Amos 5:14,15.
[246] Amos 4:1; 6:1–6.
[247] Amos 3:15.
[248] Amos 6:4. The Buddha also found the use of elevated beds a moral offense.
[249] Amos 2:8; 4:1; 6:6. They are also accused of making the Nazarites break their vow of total abstinence (2:12).

in which they indulged.[250] By implication, the lifestyle of the righteous rich will not be characterized by excess and luxury.

Amos announced God's anger about the self-centeredness of the rich and their cruelty toward others, but he was also furious at their treatment of God himself. They worshiped other gods in addition to him, thus breaking their covenant with him.[251] They substituted liturgy and offerings at feast times for daily justice.[252] They ignored the truth of God's coming judgment or deceived themselves that they had nothing to fear from the "day of the Lord."[253] They loved making money more than honoring God.[254] When a prophet had the courage to tell them the truth about themselves, they silenced him, and when the high standards of some put the rich in a bad light, they tried to corrupt them.[255] The rich became proud and boastful,[256] and saw themselves as superior to other nations.[257] They forgot the power and greatness of God and lulled themselves into a false sense of security. Therefore, we find regular reminders of the character of God in the book of Amos.[258]

The righteous rich, by contrast, live eschatologically, with an over-riding sense of God's impending judgment, and this outlook influences their whole life. There is no infidelity to God, nor any form of idolatry. Faith is not compartmentalized, but integrated with all of life. The righteous rich have the humility to learn from God's servants whose words and lifestyles point out their sins.

In the book of Amos, righteousness is justice.[259] As we have seen, this justice was directly related to the covenant relationship and the Law of God, and Amos insists that they go together. Without justice, God counted all of the sacrifices, tithes, and offerings of the rich as sin.[260] Sin calls forth judgment. Amos is largely a book about God's

---

[250] Amos 6:4–6.
[251] Amos 5:26.
[252] Amos 5:21–24.
[253] Amos, 5:18–20; 6:3; 9:10.
[254] Amos 8:5.
[255] Amos 2:11,12; 7:12,13.
[256] Amos 6:13.
[257] This attitude is implied in the way Amos brings unflattering comparisons between Israel and the nations in 2:9–12; 6:2; 9:7–9.
[258] Amos 5:8,9; 9:5,6.
[259] Note the parallelism in Amos 5:7,24; 6:12.
[260] Amos 4:4,5.

judgment upon the rich for their unrighteousness.[261] The rich who ignore the warnings of Amos are in grave spiritual, physical, and national danger.

> **But wealth has a way of blinding one's eyes to the needs of the less fortunate, of contracting the fist and hardening the heart.**

Amos was a rural prophet sent by God as a missionary to point out the sins of wealthy urbanites in a neighboring country. This was not a comfortable position. One thing which made it especially uncomfortable was that his own country was guilty of the same sins.[262] Amos did his best to soften the blow of the words he had to speak by first criticizing the sins of enemy countries and then of his native Judah. But ultimately he had the courage to deliver the message entrusted to him by God and incur the wrath of a leading priest and of the king himself.[263] It helped in this tense situation that Amos could point to his own simplicity of lifestyle and lack of profit motive in his mission.[264] Perhaps there is a lesson here.

There are righteous poor in the book of Amos,[265] but no righteous rich. This is not because prosperity is wrong. Ironically, the book closes with a promise of restoration to abundant harvests, cities to live in, and plenty of wine. But wealth has a way of blinding one's eyes to the needs of the less fortunate, of contracting the fist and hardening the heart. Amos does not command, "Sell all you have and give to the poor." He simply called for a return to righteousness: justice in court, concern for the nation, empathy for the plight of the poor, and the fear of God. The king, priests, and the well-off found such an invitation unpalatable. If Amos returned to the nations of our world today, it is likely he would encounter a similar animosity.

---

[261] These judgments are logical consequences: those who crush the poor will be crushed (2:7–13), those who take from the poor will have their own belongings taken from them (5:11), and so on.
[262] Consider the words of contemporary Isaiah to the people of Judah in Isaiah, chapters 1, 3, 5, and 10. The parallels are striking.
[263] Amos 7:10–13.
[264] Amos 7:14,15.
[265] Amos 2:6.

2

The Righteous Rich in the New Testament

Righteousness and Riches in the Sermon on the Mount

One day a rich man came to Jesus with a question about what good thing he could do to inherit eternal life. Had he been in Galilee and not in Judea, he might have anticipated Jesus' answer, because he would have had opportunity to listen to the Sermon on the Mount. This sermon, deemed by most theologians to be the essence of Jesus' ethical instruction, is primarily about righteousness, and it has a few things to say about money as well.

The introduction of the sermon focuses on the character of the one who is blessed. Among other qualities, the one upon whom God smiles is poor in spirit, hungry and thirsty for righteousness, and persecuted because of righteousness.[266] Here the link seems to be, not righteousness and riches, but the opposite—righteousness and poverty.

But what sort of poverty? There is a general agreement among commentators that being poor in spirit includes a recognition of one's indebtedness to God and dependency on him.[267] Poverty of spirit is necessarily linked with the lowliness, or "meekness," Jesus mentions two verses later.[268]

---

[266] Matthew 5:3,6,10.
[267] For example, John R. W. Stott, *Christian Counter Culture: The Message of the Sermon on the Mount* (Downers Grove: Intervarsity, 1978), 36; David Hill, *The Gospel of Matthew* from *The New Century Bible Commentary* series (Grand Rapids; Eerdmans, 1972), 111; Douglas R. A. Hare, *Matthew* from *Interpretation: A Bible Commentary for Teaching and Preaching* series, James Luther Mays, ed. (Louisville: Knox, 1993), 36–37; W. F. Albright and C. S. Mann, *Matthew* from *The Anchor Bible*, W. F. Albright and D. N. Freedman, eds. (Garden City, New York: Doubleday, 1971), 46.
[268] Matthew 5:5.

Can one be materially rich and "poor in spirit"? Matthew does not answer that question directly in his recording of the introduction to the Sermon on the Mount, but the parallel in Luke's "Sermon on the Plain" is lacking in any subtlety. "Blessed are you who are poor, . . . who hunger now. . . . Woe to you who are rich, . . . who are well fed now. . . ."[269] For Luke, in Jesus' upside-down kingdom, there is an inverse correlation between one's possessions in this age and in the age to come.

While Matthew is not so explicit, he implies at least that someone rich in this world's goods must live in a manner inconsistent with his wealth if he is to inherit the kingdom of heaven and its rewards. He must not be proud, for the meek are blessed.[270] He must not be so sated with good things that he fails to suffer pangs of hunger for righteousness.[271] He must willingly lose money to his debtors, because the merciful are blessed.[272] He must not try to serve God and money, because God blesses the pure in heart.[273] He must count the loss of his property, reputation, and ease a marvelous asset if the loss results from persecution for righteousness.[274] He must not let his wealth take the edge off his ability to glorify God by his deeds or to influence the society for good.[275]

Having touched upon poverty and righteousness in his introduction, Jesus' first main point is that righteousness consists in commitment to wholesome relationships. It answers the question, "What sort of righteousness enables one to enter the kingdom of heaven?" This, of course, is precisely the question of the rich young man who came to Jesus, and in both instances Jesus began his answer with the Law. Jesus wanted to leave no doubt that he respected the Law as the basic yardstick by which righteousness is measured. But he also wanted to leave no doubt that the righteousness of those most proficient in the Law was totally inadequate: "For I tell you that unless your righteousness surpasses that of the Pharisees and

---

[269] Luke 6:20–25.
[270] Matthew 5:5.
[271] Matthew 5:6.
[272] Matthew 5:7.
[273] Matthew 5:8; 6:24.
[274] Matthew 5:10–12; Hebrews 10:34.
[275] Matthew 5:13–16.

the teachers of the law, you will certainly not enter the kingdom of heaven."[276] Jesus had not come to annul the Law, but to teach the full extent of righteousness implied in the Law.[277]

This righteousness goes beyond mere compliance with external legal restrictions and obligations. It goes back to the idea of right relationships, which was Jesus' first main point in the sermon. The ban on murder in the Law deals only with an extreme aspect of relational breakdown. Jesus declares a greater righteousness which has no place for rage or insults, which places reconciliation above the technically correct performance of worship, and which avoids the use of the courts to solve relational problems.[278] The adultery forbidden by the Law is only the extreme expression of unrighteous lusts which should be squelched just as severely.[279] It is more righteous to preserve the marriage than to divorce according to legal form.[280] The righteous person doesn't quibble about which oath is more binding, but simply tells the truth.[281] He recognizes that right relationships will never be gained through extracting legally sanctioned revenge, and so foregoes his rights and walks the second mile for the sake of righteousness.[282] A truly righteous person will even seek the good of his enemies.[283] The primary purpose of the Law, as we discovered in our discussion of Deuteronomy, is not legislation but faithful relationships based on a covenant with God. Those who are God's children will want to go far beyond the technical requirements of the Law, just as God has done far more than obligation required. God himself is the ultimate standard of righteousness.[284]

In this portion of the sermon there is no direct reference to the rich. In fact, Jesus may have had the poor and vulnerable particularly in mind, at least for some points.[285] But there are a few teachings

---

[276] Matthew 5: 20.
[277] Matthew 5:17–19; 7:12.
[278] Matthew 5:21–26.
[279] Matthew 5:27–30.
[280] Matthew 5:31,32.
[281] Matthew 5:33–37. The original purpose of an oath was truth, and Jesus discards the form which has become distorted for the sake of the original purpose. Jesus addresses the distortion directly in Matthew 23:16–22. Particularly noteworthy in this context is the lawyers' preference for gold over the temple in v. 16.
[282] Matthew 5:38–42.
[283] Matthew 5:43–47.
[284] Matthew 5:45,48.
[285] For instance, 5:25,26,39,41. Notice also Luke's, "Blessed are *you* who are poor." (Luke 6:20)

which sit uncomfortably with many rich people. It is the people with money who are able to lend, and they are told not to refuse a loan to anyone.[286] It is the well-off who are asked most often for money, and they are told not to turn anyone down.[287] Inevitably the rich person will be faced with dilemmas in which he must choose between his money and righteousness. His actions will reveal which he craves more.[288]

Jesus dealt with this either/or dilemma directly in the Sermon on the Mount, but before he could deal with it satisfactorily, he had to address the issue of *how* acts of righteousness were to be carried out, that is, discreetly. Righteousness for reputation's sake does not count as righteousness as far as God is concerned.[289]

Jesus chose three acts of righteousness with which to illustrate his point. The first has great significance for the situation in the contemporary Middle East. Jesus said that donations given to the poor in such a way as to enhance the reputation of the donor have accomplished for the donor all they will ever accomplish.[290] One must choose between impressing people and impressing the Heavenly Father who has an eye for secret benevolence. God knows the subtle difference between a gift to another and an investment in oneself.

The prayers of the righteous should also be carried out in secret for the same reason.[291] Jesus added that righteous prayer is simple and concise, expressing confidence that the Father knows full well what the children need before they ask.[292] The model prayer he provided is very brief, expressing a desire for the kingdom of heaven and a simple request for daily bread.[293] The next sentence in the prayer pertains especially to those who have enough money to lend: "Forgive us our debts, as we also have forgiven our debtors."[294] It is clear from the verses which follow the model prayer that Jesus intended forgiveness to go well beyond canceling financial obligations.[295] But in no way does the broader sense of the petition nullify the literal meaning. The

---

[286] Matthew 5:42.
[287] Ibid.
[288] Matthew 6:19–24.
[289] Matthew 6:1.
[290] Matthew 6:2.
[291] Matthew 6:5,6.
[292] Matthew 6:7,8.
[293] Matthew 6:9–11.
[294] Matthew 6:12.
[295] Matthew 6:14,15.

righteous do not have the bad taste to ask God to dismiss their sins when they refuse to dismiss another person's debt.[296] The Greek of the parallel in Luke 11:4 is translated literally, "Forgive us our sins, for we have forgiven everyone indebted to us." It is almost as if Jesus were saying, "Canceling another's debt is the way to express your desire for God's forgiveness." Again, a person may have to choose between getting back the money he is owed and becoming righteousness.

Jesus also applies the secrecy principle to fasting.[297] Here the Master seems almost to advocate duplicity. Not only does one refrain from boasting about his fast, he goes so far as to disguise his self-denial with the appearance that he is being self-indulgent, anointing his head with oil. He can do this with integrity, because he is in fact fasting to feast on the Word of God and celebrating in advance the reward of God.[298]

Jesus' second point in the Sermon on the Mount is that genuine righteousness has no this-worldly, ulterior motives. This is a message for everyone, but it holds particular force for those who are in the public eye, people like politicians, leaders in business, and entertainers, many of whom are wealthy. It also holds for religious leaders and missionaries who might be tempted to prove the truth of their doctrine by their moral superiority. The righteous person will certainly do righteous deeds, but in such a way that people glorify God, for the glory is his.[299]

Jesus' third main point in the Sermon on the Mount is that the righteous person gives unequivocal priority to God's kingdom over his own material well-being. He points to three principles which govern the righteous person's decisions about money. Because they are so relevant to our topic, we will look at each of them.

1. *Your heart will be with what you treasure.*[300] The obvious implication is that the righteous person does not treasure things, and to avoid treasuring them, he avoids collecting them. "Storing up" implies excess beyond the necessities of life. It is very difficult to reconcile this passage with the concept of "the righteous rich." The rich

---

[296] This is the point of the parable of the unforgiving servant, Matthew 18:21–35.
[297] Matthew 6:16–18.
[298] See Matthew 4:1–4; John 4:31,32. Contrast the prophet's warning to the rich in Amos 8:11. Compare Matthew 5:12.
[299] Matthew 5:16 (and 6:13, the traditional ending of the Lord's Prayer).
[300] Matthew 6:19–21.

young man who asked Jesus how to inherit eternal life sadly turned his back on Jesus and his answer because the young man's heart was with his treasure. Jesus' reflection on the situation was, "How hard it is for a rich man to enter the kingdom of God!" If there is any possibility of reconciling wealth and godliness in this passage it is found in the words, "for yourselves."[301] Perhaps, just perhaps, a person might "lay up" treasure for others.

2. *The eye is the lamp of the body.*[302] I never understood this passage until I moved to the Middle East. Here I learned about the evil eye, the envious look that brings a curse. Fear of the evil eye is ancient and widespread throughout the Mediterranean basin, and there is no reason to doubt that Jesus was familiar with it.[303] However, in popular thinking, the envious person puts a curse on the one he envies, whereas in Jesus' teaching, the envious one brings darkness upon himself. The righteous person will be full of light because the lamp of his body is good, for he does not envy the successes of others.[304]

3. *One cannot serve both God and money.*[305] Jesus is not saying here simply that God must take priority over money in one's life. Money cannot come in a close second—not even a distant second. A person can only serve God if money has no mastery over him. This makes it very hard indeed for a rich person to enter the kingdom of heaven.

Notice that Jesus never says here that one cannot be righteous and rich. Instead he tells his disciples how life works. It may be possible to make water run uphill in certain circumstances, but that doesn't change the fact that water's tendency is downward. There may be examples of the righteous rich, but Jesus' warning is not diminished because of them.

---

[301] Gary North, "A Free Market Response" in *Wealth and Poverty: Four Christian Views of Economics*, ed. Robert G. Clouse (Downers Grove: Intervarsity, 1984), 164.
[302] Matthew 6:22,23.
[303] Consider Matthew 20:15 (in the context of the parable of the envious day-laborers) and Mark 7:22.
[304] Some consider envy one of the sins of the poor, but the rich have done their share of coveting. Think of King David and Uriah's wife (2 Samuel 11) or King Ahab and Naboth's vineyard (1 Kings 21).
[305] Matthew 6:24.

Most of us look to money as a source of security for our lives. We cannot live without it. Jesus clearly understood the fears his teaching about money would raise, and he immediately sought to alleviate those fears in his sermon. To avoid being mastered by money, one must believe in the tender care of a heavenly Father. God makes sure that the birds are fed. Fabulously wealthy Solomon in royal finery couldn't compete with the wildflowers whose garments God himself designed. Jesus reminded his hearers that God is faithful. If they seek his kingdom and his righteousness above even the basic necessities of life, God will see that their needs are looked after. Worry accomplishes nothing, and it cannot be accepted as an excuse to put our physical well-being above God's righteousness. Trust in God's righteousness and desire for it are tests of the disciple's righteousness.

Jesus, in contrasting God's righteousness to that of the Pharisees and teachers of the Law, remembers to make another warning about that unsatisfactory type of righteousness. True righteousness is not a club with which to beat others, and it cannot be forced on those who do not want it.[306] The Teacher returns to the subject of the Father's care, urging his disciples to ask God for their needs with simple, child-like expectancy.[307] Then Jesus wraps the sermon up in one sentence: the righteousness that the Law and Prophets teach can be summed up in treating others the way one wishes to be treated.

There has been much debate in the history of the church as to how the Sermon on the Mount should be interpreted. A careful inspection of the different theories is beyond the scope of this book.[308] But in his conclusion, Jesus made clear that he was not *merely* stating an ideal to make people sense their need of grace (although it certainly *is* that). He actually expected his disciples to practice the righteousness he described in the sermon.[309] It is not an optional extra for the spiritual superhero, but the narrow way

---

[306] Matthew 7:1–6.
[307] Matthew 7:7–11.
[308] For one discussion of the various approaches used to interpret the Sermon on the Mount, see Archibald M. Hunter, *The Sermon on the Mount: An Exposition of the Sermon on the Mount* (Philadelphia: Westminster, 1965), 99–106.
[309] Matthew 7:13–27; 21:28–32. It is possible that Jesus used some hyperbole, and that not everything should be taken literally such as the example about gouging out the eyes. On the other hand, Jesus never expressed any concern about the eternal fate of one so blinded, but he was clearly dismayed at the fate of some whose sight would destroy them. See also Matthew 5:29,30.

to life.[310] Much of what is dismissed verbally as not doable is in fact dismissed because we find it undesirable, and because we do not believe that God would really take care of us if we risked plunging into his righteousness.

Matthew understands righteousness as godliness in the context of right relationships.[311] Matthew never meant for the sermon to be taken as an ethical code divorced from the ministry, death, and resurrection of Jesus. From birth to the grave, rich people encountered Jesus. Jesus did not deal with them on the basis of some external rule, but on the basis of their need. Some were spiritual failures,[312] but others are clearly viewed favorably. These latter are characterized by great faith in God's care for their physical needs or by great generosity based on faith.[313]

Many people of various times and places are portrayed in Matthew as righteous.[314] One must have a superior sort of righteousness to enter the kingdom of heaven.[315] But all of this righteousness is contingent upon the person of Jesus. Jesus, says Matthew, taught with unique authority.[316] He confidently defined righteousness because he saw in himself the fulfillment of the Law and the Prophets.[317] Powerful ministries, even in Jesus' name, fail to be truly righteous apart from the knowledge of him.[318] He will be the judge of the righteous and the wicked at the final judgment, and he will reckon every righteous act as though it were done for him personally.[319] The Sermon on the Mount was preached to disciples, not the crowds.[320] It was taught to those who could call God "Father" and entrust their lives to his tender care.[321]

---

[310] Matthew 5:20; 7:13,14,19.
[311] One more example: in the explanation of the parable of the weeds, the good seeds are "the sons of the kingdom," and these "righteous will shine like the sun in the kingdom of their Father" (Matt 13:37–43).
[312] Matthew 2:3–18; 19:16–24; 23:25, for example.
[313] For great faith, see the centurion (Matt 8:5–10) and the ruler (Matt 9:18). For generosity, go to the Magi (Matt 2:1–12) and to Joseph of Arimathea (Matt 27:57–60).
[314] Matthew 10:41; 13:17,43; 23:35.
[315] Matthew 5:20.
[316] Matthew 7:28,29.
[317] Matthew 5:17; 3:13–17.
[318] Matthew 7:21–23.
[319] Matthew 25:31–40.
[320] Matthew 5:1,2.
[321] Matthew 6:8,9,32.

Jesus' execution was somehow the summation of all the murders of the righteous from the beginning of creation.[322] It is only in the context of the righteousness of Jesus and its ultimate expression in the cross that the Sermon on the Mount can be fully appreciated and appropriated. The Sermon on the Mount was never intended by Jesus to be followed apart from a relationship with him, a relationship made possible by his sacrifice. For all the stress the sermon lays on human responsibility, its lofty standards were not proclaimed by Moses, but by Jesus, the one who would save his people from their sin.[323]

"I will be with you always."[324] It is in Jesus' presence that Christ-followers proclaim what they have learned from Jesus. In the light of his resurrection, Jesus' unparalleled authority sends his followers into the world to "make disciples, baptizing them . . . and teaching them to obey everything I have commanded you." What Jesus has commanded includes a great deal about wealth and righteousness.

The Acts of the Apostles and the Church in Jerusalem

We cannot be sure of the prosperity of Joseph, also called Barnabas, but he is probably the best example of "the righteous rich" in the record of the Jerusalem church. We have three hints that he was well-situated: he owned land he felt he could dispose of,[325] he traveled extensively,[326] and his near relative, Mary, was wealthy, for she owned a house large enough to function as a meeting place and she kept a servant.[327] About his righteousness, the book of Acts leaves us in no doubt. Despite the unsatisfying last mention of him in Acts 15:39, Luke was clearly impressed with Barnabas' boldness, farsighted

---

[322] Matthew 23:34–36. It is easy to miss the profound Christological and soteriological implications of these verses.
[323] Matthew 1:21.
[324] Matthew 28:19,20.
[325] Acts 4:36,37.
[326] Acts 4:36; 11:25,26,29,30; 13:2–4; 13:13,50,51; 14:6,20,21,24–26; 15:2,3,30; 15:39; Galatians 2:1; 1 Corinthians 16:5–7. Travel itself was not necessarily a sign of wealth in the Roman Empire with its excellent roads and abundant means of transport, but the last-mentioned reference indicates that Paul and Barnabas paid their own way, in contrast to the other apostles. Both men worked of necessity (note 1 Cor 9:6), and from this we may conclude that they were not vastly wealthy. Nonetheless, travel was time-consuming and costly, and it is likely that both men drew upon reserves.
[327] Acts 12:12,13. Perhaps a fourth piece of evidence is the ease with which Barnabas and Saul gained the ear of the proconsul in Barnabas' native Cyprus.

leadership, integrity, godliness, passion for truth, and generosity. But these qualities were not unique to Barnabas. They were characteristic of the ordinary members of the Jerusalem church in its earliest days. In this section we will consider the environment in which the faith of Barnabas was nurtured, and its contribution to the biblical concept of "the righteous rich."

Following the promise of the Holy Spirit and the ascension of our Lord, 120 believers made their first order of business the replacing of Judas, who destroyed himself after committing great wickedness for financial reward.[328] Peter specifically draws attention to a field, "The Field of Blood," which was purchased with the money he received for his treachery.[329] It may be that the evil act of Judas and its evil motivation served as an incentive to the fledgling community of faith to do just the opposite: to follow Jesus faithfully with boldness, transparency, and a commitment to share money rather than acquire it.

A sense of eschatological anticipation pervades the early chapters of Acts. The disciples want to know when the kingdom will be restored to Israel.[330] A hundred and twenty believers make it their highest priority to bring the number of apostles back to twelve. When the Holy Spirit is poured out dramatically on the believers, Peter began his explanation to the confused crowds of on-lookers with the assertion that eschatological prophecy was being fulfilled. It is not surprising, then, that those who had been filled by the Spirit expressed their transformation in ways consistent with the eschatological ideals of the Law and the Prophets. These included the hope that there would no longer be any poor, and that the disabled would be made whole, and that the poor would have the good news preached to them.[331]

---

[328] Acts 1:18. The Gospels are also explicit about the role money played in the downfall of Judas. See Matthew 26:14–16; Mark 14:10,11; Luke 22:4,5; John 12:4–6; 13:26–30.

[329] There are echoes of Cain in the tragic story of Judas. And, as at the Exodus, the Hebrew slaves finally received some of their deserved pay through the "loan" of their masters' finery, so the poor would receive through Judas' tragic death some compensation, in the form of a pauper's graveyard, for the cash Judas had pilfered from the disciples' collection for the poor (John 12:6).

[330] Acts 1:6. See also 3:21.

[331] Compare Deuteronomy 15:4 with Acts 4:34; Isaiah 35:6 with Acts 3:8; and Isaiah 61:1–3 with Acts 2:14–3:26 and 6:1–10.

The Holy Spirit filled the believing community with unity and wonder. Luke describes the awesome mood of it all in Acts 2:42–47 and 4:32–35. Perhaps the greatest miracle of all was the willingness of people to share their wealth and belongings so freely among one another. No doubt there were some who had come to Jerusalem[332] on pilgrimage or business who prolonged their stay to benefit from the apostle's teaching and the fellowship of the community. These would have needed hospitality. Among the many new converts were a considerable number of widows who relied on other believers for the essentials of life.[333] In addition, since Jerusalem was the preferred place in which Jews would give alms, the city was full of the sick, deranged, disabled, and destitute looking for hand-outs.[334] Luke reports that crowds of this sort were attracted to the healing powers of the apostles.[335] Given the tremendous needs, it would have been natural for the wealthier members of the believing community to conceal and guard their possessions lest they be overwhelmed with calls upon their generosity. This they did not do. Instead, they opened their homes and their hearts. "No one claimed that any of his possessions was his own, but they shared everything they had."[336]

The church in Jerusalem did respect the right to private property. For example, Mary the sister of Barnabas did not give up her house or her maid. Nonetheless, what they achieved has rarely been duplicated. What is more, a number of people went beyond the giving of alms, the ungrudging sharing of ready cash, and the selling of possessions. Some donated their means of income and economic security: land. The "son of Encouragement" (Barnabas) is specifically mentioned in this regard. He sold a field and submissively placed the proceeds at the apostles' feet.[337] What a contrast to Judas!

Luke's explicit contrast is not between Barnabas and Judas, however, but between Barnabas and the couple Ananias and Sapphira.[338] They also sold a field, agreed secretly to keep back

---

[332] See Acts 2:5–11.
[333] See Acts 6:1 and also the example of Dorcas in Joppa in Acts 9:36–39.
[334] Joachim Jeremias, *Jerusalem in the Time of Jesus* (Philadelphia: Fortress, 1969),116–119.
[335] Acts 5:15,16.
[336] Acts 4:32b.
[337] Acts 4:36,37.
[338] Acts 5:1–11. The chapter break between 4:37 and 5:1 is ill-placed and obscures the obvious contrast.

part of the proceeds for themselves, and presented the rest to the apostles as though it were the full sum. Peter accused them of lying to and testing the Holy Spirit, and each of the two was struck dead with bone-chilling suddenness. The message was clear: these were emphatically *not* models of the righteous rich.

What offense merited such drastic punishment by God? Although the text does not say so explicitly, it is likely that the unhappy couple had made a vow to sell the field and donate it, since this was common practice in Judaism. The language of Peter in Acts 5:4 certainly reflects Old Testament warnings about the paying of vows.[339] If a vow had been made, then their sin was essentially that of Achan who attempted to keep for himself what ought to have been devoted to God. As though this were not enough, the deception that Ananias and Sapphira practiced displayed a disdain for God's omniscience and love of truth. The lie revealed hypocrisy, desire for human praise, a grudging attitude toward the needs of the community of faith, and a disrespect for the apostles as Jesus' designated authorities. Had Ananias and Sapphira been successful in lying about the price of the field, they would have undermined the credibility of the Holy Spirit's power and the trust and unity of the church at the crucial time of its formation. The well-being of the people of God depended on their transparency and open-handedness in financial matters.

One of the advantages of the system of donations practiced by the early believers in Jerusalem was that it reduced the extent to which donors could manipulate recipients to gain power and honor. All gifts were channeled through the apostles. Ananias and Sapphira may have resented not receiving what were considered at the time the rights of benefactors.[340]

The duplicity of Ananias and Sapphira is tacitly contrasted with the integrity of the apostles in money matters. Large sums were being laid at their feet,[341] indicating that the apostles were being given total authority in the use of it. They could easily have

---

[339] For example, Deuteronomy 23:21–23; Ecclesiastes 5:1–7. Another interesting passage in light of the rejection of Ananias and Sapphira is Psalm 15 (especially v.4).

[340] Moxnes, Halvar, "Patron-Client Relations and the New Community in Luke-Acts," in *The Social World of Luke-Acts: Models for Interpretation*, Jerome H. Neyrey, ed. (Peabody, Mass.: Hendrickson, 1991), 264–266.

[341] Acts 4:34,35.

justified spending it to enrich themselves as the ones chosen by the Messiah to govern the new Israel, but they did no such thing. Peter put it succinctly to the lame man, "Silver and gold I do not have."[342] The apostles took very seriously the responsibility of supporting the widows. When accused of organizational mismanagement of the charitable fund for widows, the apostles turned the administration over to others,[343] thus demonstrating their humility, their integrity, and their confidence that the Spirit was at work in the non-apostles. The twelve, who had unique authority given by Christ, who were performing amazing miracles, and who had thousands hanging on their every word, were not above being held accountable by the Greek-speaking Jews. In fact they allowed the believers to choose a seven-man committee composed entirely of Greek-speakers,[344] despite the fact that they themselves were Hebraic. They refused to use donated money to enhance their power base, to favor their sub-group, or to keep people dependent upon them personally.

Although the early chapters of Acts provide no explicit teaching about righteous rich people, a number of clear inferences can be drawn from the life of the church in Jerusalem. The righteous rich will not behave treacherously or deceitfully in order to gain or retain money. They will be honest about their financial dealings, keep their vows, allow themselves to be held accountable, and entrust money matters to godly, responsible others. They will give sacrificially and humbly to meet the needs of the poor, and especially the widows within the church. They will not consider their belongings their own as much as they consider their belongings means by which to serve others. They will open their homes. They will give whenever they see need. They will do all these things because they are filled with the Holy Spirit and fully integrated into the life of the church with its truth, power, fellowship, joy, and awe. Luke gives no command concerning wealth, but he paints glowing descriptions of the Jerusalem church, and fearful portrayals of what money did to Judas, Ananias, and Sapphira. In so doing, he raises the bar to a considerable height.

---

[342] Acts 3:6.
[343] Acts 6:1–6.
[344] Acts 6:1–6.

James and the Unrighteous Rich

James has nothing to say about the righteous rich, even though he refers by name to both Abraham and Job.[345] Biblical regard for the rich reaches rock bottom in his letter. This is not because of any Platonism on James' part. God is the source of every good and perfect gift and the healer of the body.[346] It would appear that James' antipathy toward the rich is based on what he and his readers have experienced of the rich.[347] He draws on the traditions of the prophets in his denunciations. As we did with our study of Amos, we shall have to content ourselves with learning from James what the righteous rich are not.

For James, wealth and pride are Siamese twins. So James begins his address to the rich by sarcastically urging them to take pride in their low estate.[348] The sarcasm is evident in that he gives them absolutely nothing of which to be proud. Instead, he waxes poetical about how quickly they will fade and die, even while going about their business.[349] The rich think that they are in control of their lives, and so they boast of their travel and mercenary plans without taking into account God's sovereignty over their lives and abilities.[350]

James chides the readers for buying into the positive discrimination which the rich have come to expect without regard to its effect on the poor.[351] It is interesting to note why James opposes this discrimination. First, it is a source of divisions among the brothers. Second, it puts the one who does the discriminating in the seat of the judge, and there is only One who has the right to judge.[352] Third, not only are those who discriminate judges, but they are "judges with evil thoughts."[353] Normally a judge with evil thoughts is committing an injustice in order to benefit financially. Could it be that those who arranged the seating in Christian gatherings hoped to gain favors for themselves by their fawning behavior? Perhaps this was the

---

[345] James 2:23; 5:11.
[346] James 1:17; 5:14–16.
[347] James 2:6.
[348] James 1:10.
[349] James 1:11; 5:1–3.
[350] James 4:13–17.
[351] James 2:1–4.
[352] James 4:11,12.
[353] James 2:4

case, for James warns members of the congregations against selfish ambition and the greedy squabbling that has disturbed their unity and sullied their relationship with God.[354] Favoritism toward the rich in something as simple as seating arrangements is for James an issue of justice. Finally, pushing the poor aside for the sake of the rich is a failure to obey God's law, a law which requires love for the neighbor to be like love for oneself.[355] To fulfill God's law is to empathize with the poor person and treat him as an equal.

James assumes ill of the rich as a class, and rails against them indiscriminately.[356] The poor person is a "brother" and can take pride in his high position.[357] "Listen, my dear brothers and sisters: Has not God chosen those who are poor in the eyes of the world to be rich in faith and to inherit the kingdom he promised those who love him?"[358] But the rich are not addressed as brothers at all. James records their sins in detail. They exploit others, and particularly their own agricultural laborers.[359] The rich have no mercy, but drag people to court, condemn them unjustly, and even have them killed—people who have not done them any wrong.[360] That they are not fellow believers is evident from their blasphemy.[361] They do not acknowledge that God is the one who determines their fate.[362] The rich hoard wealth and live in luxury and self-indulgence.[363] Their doom is dreadful and sure.[364]

The righteous, by contrast, live eschatologically, awaiting their vindication with the patience of Job.[365] They are lowly or humble,

---

[354] James 3:14,16; 4:1–4.
[355] James 2:8,9. Here James quotes Leviticus 19:18.
[356] James 1:10; 5:1–6.
[357] James 1:9. According to Countryman, the motif of the pious poor had infused all of Christian tradition well before A. D. 66. See L. Wm. Countryman, *The Rich Christians in the Church of the Early Empire: Contradictions and Accommodations* (New York: Edwin Mellen Press, 1980), 32.
[358] James 2:5. Note again the use of the word "brothers" at the start of this verse.
[359] James 2:6; 5:4. It was not uncommon among Jewish communities at the time for rich oppressors also to act as patrons to the poor to create bonds of gratitude and to act as a control mechanism. Oakman, Douglas E., "The Countryside in Luke-Acts," in *The Social World of Luke-Acts: Models for Interpretation* (Neyrey, Jerome H., editor. Peabody, Mass.: Hendrickson, 1991), 159.
[360] James 2:6; 5:6.
[361] James 2:7.
[362] James 4:13,14.
[363] James 5:3,5.
[364] James 1:10,11; 5:1–5.
[365] James 5:7–11. Notice that it is Job's perseverance in poverty, rather than his righteous behavior in riches, which James finds worthy of emulation. The virtue of perseverance under trial is also praised in 1:12.

and God gives them grace.[366] They submit their lives and hopes to God's control, saying, "If it is the Lord's will, we will live and do this or that."[367] They do not deceive themselves with a practice of outward religion divorced from inner purity and social conscience.[368] They control their tongues.[369] Their wisdom and peace-making result in a harvest of righteousness.[370] Their prayers of faith are powerful like Elijah's.[371] The righteous person gives practical, physical care to the poor.[372]

For James, righteousness is faith in action. Abraham is his primary model of righteousness.[373] James is at pains to point out that Abraham's righteousness was not credited to him simply on the basis of intellectual assent to dogma, but on the basis of a living faith that revealed itself in concrete action. In Abraham's case, it was the offering of his dear son Isaac on the altar which demonstrated his righteousness.

No commentary on James can avoid the issue of the contrast between James' use of the Abraham story and Paul's use of the same story in Romans 4. Paul teaches imputed righteousness, not righteousness attained through strict observance of the Jewish legal code. This is why he so stresses the point that Abraham was reckoned as righteous before he was circumcised. James, on the other hand, is not concerned about the role of the Mosaic Law, but about hypocrisy. He is arguing against what appears to be a distortion of Pauline teaching, that faith consists merely of mental assent to true propositions about God. James insists that Abraham's righteousness was not merely imputed, but actual as well. Whereas Paul focuses on the moment of Abraham's confidence in God's unlikely promise, and shows from the Scriptures that this was sufficient for him to be "credited as righteous," James takes the same phrase and treats it as a prophecy which is both inherently true and in need of fulfillment.

---

[366] James 1:9,21; 4:6.
[367] James 4:15. Such was Paul's habit—see Acts 18:21; Romans 1:10; 15:32; 1 Corinthians 4:19.
[368] James 1:22,26,27.
[369] James 1:19,20,26; 3:1–12.
[370] James 3:17,18.
[371] James 5:15–18.
[372] James 1:27; 2:14–17.
[373] James 2:20–24. His secondary example, after the venerable "Father of the Jews," is Rahab, a Gentile prostitute.

The fulfillment of Abraham's faith (and thus his righteousness) came with the offering up of Isaac. Abraham believed God had the power to do what he had promised, "and it was credited to him as righteousness."[374] He proved that his faith was effective in his life, and that the righteousness God accredited to him was genuine by raising the knife over Isaac on Mount Horeb.[375]

Both writers believe that righteousness is born from a relationship with God based on faith. Both writers believe that faith must be worked out in practice for the believer: it is those who do the Law who are called righteous, not merely those who hear it.[376] The difference is one of emphasis: in Romans, Paul stresses imputed righteousness as being primary and essential (as against Law-based righteousness), whereas James lays his accent on extrinsic righteousness which is necessary to confirm that one's faith is effectual. Accordingly, Paul refers frequently to the cross in Romans, but seldom to Jesus' ethical teachings. James is confident that his hearers have the basics of Christian theology, but is dubious about its power in their daily lives.[377] He makes several references to Jesus' ethical teachings.[378]

In his letter to the Jewish diaspora, James contrasts the terms "righteous" and "rich," drawing on Jesus and the prophets who made the same contrast. Any person who genuinely wants to know what the Bible teaches about "the righteous rich" has to reckon with the possibility that their study might conclude that no such person exists, or that such a person exists as an anomaly only. Certainly the person who wishes to be both rich and righteous has much to take warning from in the letter of James. James does not say outright that it is impossible to have "pure religion" and money, but the guidelines for living laid down in his letter would whittle away at wealth: living eschatologically, equal treatment for the lowly, mercy, financial assistance to the needy, integrity in business, and humility. When my husband and I joined our mission agency, we were told, "The only way you can come out of MECO with

---

[374] Romans 4:20–22.
[375] For James, righteousness is the result of *tested* faith. See James 1:2.
[376] Romans 2:13.
[377] James 2:1,19. James also assumes that his readers are familiar with the Hebrew Scriptures. Some of the direct references to Jesus' teachings can be found in James 3:18; 5:1,12,15.
[378] References to Jesus' teachings can be found in James 2:5; 3:18; 4:11,12; 5:1–3,9,12,15.

a small fortune is if you come in with a large one." Perhaps this is true of the Christian life. But to suffer such a loss in the way of righteousness is no loss whatever.

The Righteous Rich in 1 Timothy

Unlike James, Paul expressed in his letter to Timothy[379] confidence that the wealthy could live wholesome Christian lives awaiting the return of the Lord.[380] Yet he shared with James an unease about the effects of wealth on personal piety and on relationships within the church. To understand Paul's concerns, we need to understand the predominant Gentile culture in Greco-Roman cities. The people among whom Timothy served were sophisticated pagans by background with little ability in Old Testament hermeneutics.[381] They naturally assumed the social structure of their own society when ordering church life. Because of its similarities to contemporary Middle Eastern cultures, I will go into considerable detail about the role of the wealthy in Greco-Roman society.

The contemporary Western world has grown accustomed to the idea that the government is responsible for such things as saving the poor from destitution and building public facilities to enhance the cultural, recreational, and social life of its citizens. It was not so in the first century in the Roman Empire. Of course, a governor might choose to do these things from his own private funds or from public monies.[382] In so doing, he enhanced his popularity and his chances of staying in office. Other wealthy people might also aspire to gain influence, popularity, and political office through acts of public beneficence.[383] Thousands of ancient Greco-Roman inscriptions still announce today that such-and-such a leading Roman citizen donated this drinking fountain, that temple or stadium, these baths, or those grand statues.[384] The donations were selected with care.

---

[379] I accept the Pauline authorship of this book. However, whether or not the author was Paul has little bearing on the information presented here. The basic structures of family and society being addressed remained similar or were gradually exaggerated during the second century AD.
[380] 1 Timothy 6:17–19.
[381] 1 Timothy 1:6–8. For a picture of the religious scene in Ephesus, read Acts 19.
[382] Moxnes, "Patron-Client Relations," 249.
[383] Reggie M. Kidd, *Wealth and Beneficence in the Pastoral Epistles: A "Bourgeois" Form of Early Christianity?* (Atlanta: Scholars Press, 1990), 49.
[384] Kidd, *Wealth and Beneficence,* 88, and Moxnes, "Patron-Client Relations," 251.

If you needed the support of the intellectuals, a library might be founded. Lavish sacrifices at a religious festival would not only appease the gods, but might also win you the backing of their priests. The masses would chant your praises if you provided bread and circuses,[385] but if you were seeking office, erecting a public hall could be necessary to convince the governor of your suitability.

Sometimes these generous contributions to society came from genuine philanthropy, but the pay-backs were big enough to cloud anyone's motives.[386] Gifts which made the population more content also made the government more secure, and the donor could expect the friendship and accommodating influence of those in authority. A relatively small gift to a poor family in their time of need could buy the donor life-long loyalty and advocacy among a class of people with whom he or she had little contact. Helping others in one's time of prosperity could well lead to a reciprocal arrangement, should family fortunes turn.[387] Many benefactors were motivated by intangible rewards: glory, honor, and the "immortality" of being remembered with gratitude long after their deaths.[388]

This system of patronage in return for loyalty and honor permeated the culture, and not only at a political level. There were many voluntary societies in the Roman Empire into which people gathered themselves based on philosophical convictions, religion, ethnicity, common political views, and the like.[389] These societies, or clubs, took it upon themselves to look after the needs of their members and their members' families. While all members were required to contribute what they could, the well-off were expected to do more than others, and in return were usually given special honors, privileges, and positions of authority within the club.[390]

---

[385] The attempt of the people to make Jesus king following the feeding of the 5,000 makes a great deal of sense in the light of this Roman custom, especially when combined with the prevalent Jewish messianic expectations. Why else would Jesus give away so much food, if he wasn't seeking a popular following?

[386] Kidd, *Wealth and Beneficence*, 54.

[387] Ibid, 117.

[388] Paul praises precisely these three motives in Romans 2:5–7 as leading to eternal life in the day of "God's righteous judgment" in which he "will give to each person according to what he has done." Kidd gives a list of some of the virtues for which patrons were praised by themselves and others in inscriptions in Kidd, *Wealth and Beneficence*, 88, f.n. 177.

[389] Wayne A. Meeks, *The First Urban Christians: The Social World of the Apostle Paul* (New Haven: Yale, 1983), 77–78.

[390] Ibid, 78.

Sometimes wealthy patrons from outside the voluntary society would make donations in order to gain membership, standing, or the right to meddle in the affairs of the society. If the interest group were sufficiently small or lacking in funds, an ambitious person of even modest wealth could carve out a niche for himself or herself through patronage. The words, "or herself," are significant because women inherited equally with men under Roman law, and some wealthy women made use of their wealth to gain influence or a reputation for generosity.[391] Women were frequently patrons of Roman clubs and societies.[392]

The head of a household was also, if he chose to be, the patron of that family, using his money and connections to benefit the entire household.[393] This included not only his blood relatives, but also resident servants, slaves, and people incorporated into the family as long-term guests or adopted children. In return for his liberality and advocacy, the members of the household would grant the head their loyalty and respect, and would do what they could to protect his reputation and interests.

A Westerner unused to the patron-client system might look at it with cynicism as a rather mercenary way to run relationships. It may be helpful to remember that, although not the ideal, a great deal of this sort of thing in fact happens in our own cultures. For example, an American who is having trouble with the IRS or the INS can contact his or her senator, who will look into the problem and try to influence a solution favorable to the constituent. The senator is not required to offer this service, but re-election depends upon satisfied voters. Likewise, in our societies, most of the funding for the arts depends on wealthy patrons, the majority of whom hope for some return, if only a little brass plaque or a "thank you" in the program.

---

[391] Paul had at least one unpleasant encounter with these influential women (Acts 13:50), and led others of them to faith in Jesus (Acts 17:4,12). The New Testament mentions several women who offered their homes for hospitality or meetings, among them Mary (Acts 12:12), Lydia (Acts 16:11–15), Chloe (1 Corinthians 1:11), and "the chosen lady" (2 John 1,5,10). Although in a Semitic context, Jesus also had female patrons among his followers (Luke 8:1–3; 23:49 as well as Martha and Mary).

[392] Meeks, *The First Urban Christians,* 23–25 and Moxnes, "Patron-Client Relations," 261–263. Moxnes writes specifically about women as clients and benefactors in Luke-Acts, including within the church.

[393] Kidd discusses the work of other scholars relating the household arrangement to the structure of the church in Kidd, *Wealth and Beneficence,* 78–80.

Even in the family, it is unthinkable that one member elects not to give any Christmas gifts if all the others are doing so. Every society has a system of mutual benefit. However, the patron-client system does make the society especially vulnerable to the evils of hypocrisy (pretending that one's giving is disinterested), and corruption.[394] Beneficiaries of the system were prone to attitudes of entitlement: if you want my goodwill, give me benefits. What has all of this to do with the epistle we call 1 Timothy?

Paul wrote his first letter to Timothy urging him to stay put in Ephesus, a leading Greco-Roman city in what is now Turkey.[395] It seems that a strong hand was needed to control certain unhealthy tendencies which were developing in the church there.[396] Some of these problems of the church in Ephesus sprang directly from the involvement of wealthy persons and the prevailing patron-client assumptions of the members, rich or poor.[397]

The church in Ephesus provided regular support for widows. It certainly would have needed the generosity of its wealthy members,[398] people who would have been rewarded in society for their generosity with authority, honor, and kickbacks. How difficult it would be to deny them leadership positions—even if they were incompetent in teaching and interpreting Scripture, administrative tasks, basic morality, and family life.[399] They might be tempted to use their position of power to bend the rules for the sake of family members.[400] They might think that their contributions should eventually be repaid with interest; that they could make money

---

[394] Ananias and Sapphira succumbed to the temptation of hypocrisy in giving, and their failure could well be related to the patron-client system we are describing here. However, their unique situation as Hebraic Jews living in Jerusalem makes me reluctant to assume they had the same motives as pagans might in other parts of the Empire.
[395] 1 Timothy 1:3.
[396] The following verses demonstrate that Paul wanted Timothy to take a strong hand: 1:3; 4:11,12; 5:20; 6:17,18. Nevertheless, Timothy was to show respect for his seniors without compromising his message, and to resist any temptation to use his position to take advantage of the younger women (5:1,2).
[397] Kidd, *Wealth and Beneficence*, 75–77, in a discussion of Countryman's findings.
[398] If the amount they invested in occult items is any indication, there were some very wealthy believers in Ephesus. See Acts 19:19. Some Ephesians had enviable amounts of precious metals, gems, and fine clothing, according to Acts 20:33 and 1 Timothy 2:9.
[399] This is precisely what took place, according to L. Wm. Countryman, *The Rich Christians in the* Church, 1980. Hence the warnings and instructions of 1 Timothy 1:3–7; 3:1–12; 4:7,11–16; 6:3–5. It is in this last reference that the connection between wealth and unsound teaching becomes explicit.
[400] 1 Timothy 5:8.

while appearing to be generous.[401] If they did not get the financial or social rewards that they had hoped for from their giving, they might feel used and stop giving altogether. Dealing with sin among the wealthy members of the congregation would be a delicate matter. The wealthy women might dress in ways that drew attention to themselves and intimidated others, or they might assume that they had the right to take charge of meetings and teach, despite their corrupt doctrine and immoral lifestyles.[402] These women might even use their financial independence for self-indulgence rather than for the self-giving of motherhood.[403] They might assume that their patronage entitled them to place an elderly dependent on the list of those for whom the church provided financially.[404] How was young Timothy to handle this touchy situation?

Paul gave Timothy instructions. His first concern was sound teaching.[405] Being an overseer of the family of God, Paul affirmed, was a noble aspiration, and worthy of honor,[406] but the leader had to be able to teach.[407] He couldn't just waffle on in pompous arrogance about Jewish religious folklore, interpretations of the law that had nothing to do with the gospel, or the latest Gnostic secrets.[408] Timothy himself was to be an example that the honor of teaching the church was based on spiritual authority of clear focus, accurate doctrine, spiritual gifting, and proven character.[409] Elders engaged in preaching and teaching should be paid, presumably so that their selection would not be limited to the independently wealthy.[410]

Paul instructed Timothy in no uncertain terms that a basic level of morality was to be required of all the church leadership.[411] The fact that Paul felt it necessary to write that alcoholics should not be selected as overseers or deacons[412] suggests that the selection

---

[401] 1 Timothy 6:5.
[402] 1 Timothy 2:9–12. See Kidd, *Wealth and Beneficence*, 102–103. For Paul's perception of some of these Ephesian women, see 2 Timothy 3:6,7.
[403] 1 Timothy 2:15; 5:11–15.
[404] 1 Timothy 5:16.
[405] 1 Timothy 1:3–7.
[406] 1 Timothy 3:1; 5:17.
[407] 1 Timothy 3:2.
[408] 1 Timothy 1:3–11; 6:3–5, 20.
[409] 1 Timothy 1:5; 4:6,7,11–16.
[410] 1 Timothy 5:17,18.
[411] 1 Timothy 3.
[412] 1 Timothy 3:3,8.

process at the time of writing was based on something other than spiritual, social, and administrative suitability. Money was likely one of the corrupting factors. Henceforth, deacons would have to be tested before being confirmed in office.[413] New converts would be barred from leadership lest they became conceited.[414] Meekness and gentleness were to be encouraged among those with authority.[415] Elders would be held accountable for their sins and rebuked publicly if the accusation could be verified.[416] Not only was the leader expected to keep himself above reproach, but also to rear his children in reverence and manage his household well.[417] Even being recognized as a legitimate recipient of the widow's fund was contingent upon genuine need and long-standing evidence of a humble, godly life.[418] The message was clear: the rich were not to be given special privileges and authority inconsistent with their character.

Paul particularly tells Timothy to warn leaders against the love of money, "a root of all the evils."[419] The previous verse, describing the trap of wealth, probably refers to those who are determined to maintain their wealth.[420] The Bible records in three different places, on three different occasions, Paul's concern that the leaders and other members of the Ephesian church work hard for the sake of meeting the needs of others in the fellowship.[421] It would seem that some of the community who could work avoided doing so by abusing the system of benevolence or by outright theft.[422] Some even thought they could get rich through their good works, although Paul does not specify how.[423]

In advising Timothy about these difficulties, Paul lays down some important principles related to wealth and righteousness. Those less well-off, particularly slaves, were not to exploit the patronage of

---

[413] 1 Timothy 3:10.
[414] 1 Timothy 3:6. Paul saw a particular propensity for arrogance in the rich: 1 Timothy 6:17.
[415] 1 Timothy 3:3; 6:1; 2 Timothy 2:25. Kidd finds these texts reminiscent of the Greek eulogies of patrons (Kidd, *Wealth and Beneficence*, 90–91).
[416] 1 Timothy 5:19,20.
[417] 1 Timothy 3:4,5,12.
[418] 1 Timothy 5:3–10.
[419] 1 Timothy 6:9,10. The literal translation is my own. It seems to me that Paul did not intend to portray love of money as the only source of sin, but as an all-pervading source.
[420] Kidd, *Wealth and Beneficence*, 96.
[421] Acts 20:34,35, Ephesians 4:28; 1 Timothy 6:17,18.
[422] Ephesians 4:28; 1 Timothy 3:3,8; 5:8.
[423] 1 Timothy 6:5.

fellow believers, but to treat them with respect.[424] No one should love money or try to get rich.[425] Contentment with godliness gives a better profit than trying to gain and be godly.[426] The love of money is a root of all the evils, and the risks and temptations facing those who want to get rich are too great to make the effort worthwhile.[427] So great are the dangers of acquiring wealth that Paul warned Timothy to run away from them, and instead to run after righteousness.[428] Timothy was to grasp eternal life which, Paul explained seven verses later, was accomplished through a wealth of good deeds, generosity, and willingness to share.[429] Lest Timothy be distracted, Paul reminded him of his first calling.[430] Lest he be intimidated by the age or position of those he must oppose, his apostolic mentor reminded him of the one to whom he is answerable, the immortal and almighty Sovereign.[431]

To the wealthy, Paul urged humility, eschatological hope, and persistent generosity.[432] The humility was needed so that they could be corrected, even by their social inferiors. The eschatological hope was necessary to remind them that the financial losses they experienced for Christ would be more than reimbursed.[433] Their generosity had to be persistent in view of the constant demands on own their resources, the tendency of some to take advantage, and the fact that in the church the rich were not to expect the same kudos and kickbacks they would have received in the world for the same liberality.[434] God who gives all things richly for our enjoyment was the model of the generosity to which they must aspire.[435]

And so the epistle ends, with a challenge to rich believers to open their hands to others in order to grasp eternal life. In certain circles it is fashionable to pit the views of Paul and Jesus against each other. On this matter, at least, the two concur wholeheartedly.

---

[424] In addition to passages mentioned earlier, Paul singles out slaves in this regard (1 Timothy 6:1,2).
[425] 1 Timothy 6:8–10.
[426] 1 Timothy 6:6–8.
[427] 1 Timothy 6:9,10
[428] 1 Timothy 6:11.
[429] 1 Timothy 6:12,18,19.
[430] 1 Timothy 6:12.
[431] 1 Timothy 6:13–16. Two other doxologies are found in this short letter, both in the context of a demand for proper faith and morality in the church (1 Timothy 1:17–20; 3:14–16).
[432] 1 Timothy 6:17–19.
[433] 1 Timothy 6:19. Note also the use of the term "inheritance" in Acts 20:32.
[434] Kidd, *Wealth and Beneficence*, 131–132.
[435] 1 Timothy 6:17. There is no Platonism or asceticism whatever in this verse, nor in 4:3,4.

Conclusion

Having considered some of the key pieces about wealth and righteousness in the biblical mosaic, what are we to conclude? The pieces are uneven, having been designed and inserted in varying times and cultural contexts, and it would be a mistake to try to force them to conform to a single, simple image. Yet there are patterns.

All of the biblical writers we have studied acknowledge that wealth comes from God, the giver of all good things. God sometimes rewards and blesses his righteous ones with earthly well-being and prosperity, including wealth. He so blessed Abraham, Job, and Solomon, but not without testing them.

Wide economic disparity within the community of faith threatens to be a source of spiritual and social disintegration. The poor are not to be forced into no-win situations in which they become permanently unable to improve their situation. Blind justice should not favor the rich. The wealthy are required to help the poor and show them costly compassion. Patronage is a noble option, but one that carries with it the danger of manipulating the poor, and serving the self-interest of the rich. The wealthy and those who manage the community's money must be held accountable. They will certainly be made to account for their use of money on the Last Day.

> A rich person lives in grave spiritual danger... The wealthy can greatly reduce these spiritual risks by acknowledging God as the source and Lord of all, by trusting him without anxiety, and by opening their hearts and pockets freely to meet the needs of others.

A rich person lives in grave spiritual danger. Among the perils he or she faces are the soul-destroying temptations to hoard, to become hard-hearted and tight-fisted, to exploit the vulnerability of others, to turn a blind eye to the plight of the needy, to trust in riches, to become deaf to the call of God, to forget that God is the giver and owner of it all, to indulge in worldly pursuits and excesses, to give in order to gain prestige or position, to act arrogantly toward those of lower status, and to flaunt what they have. The wealthy can greatly reduce these spiritual risks by acknowledging God as the source and Lord of all, by trusting him without anxiety, and by opening their hearts and pockets freely to meet the needs of others. Parents among the righteous rich will devote themselves to teaching their children the wisdom of godliness by word and lifestyle.

God's law gives guidance about how to live a righteous and prosperous life, but it is not to be interpreted as a mere list of rules to be enforced by the community. True righteousness will go beyond the precise requirements of the law because it blossoms forth from a relationship with God in which God's generous character is infused into the affections and behaviors of his righteous one.

Introducing the Interviewees

Meet the experts, the people who understand the thinking and values of the Middle East from the inside. These women and men come from nine countries, from very poor to moderately wealthy families, ranging in age at the time of their interview from seventeen to fifty-eight, representing Sunni, Shi'ite, Druze, Orthodox, Catholic, and Protestant communities. Many chose to use pseudonyms. Some are quoted more than others.

Abram: student from Sudan
Abu Nader and Umm Nader: lower-class Shi'ites from the southern suburbs of Beirut
Ahmad: middle-class Sunni businessman and family man from Beirut.
Ammar: single Christian from rural Sudan
Andrea: from South Sudan
Amjad: Protestant pastor from Iraq, son of Armenian and Assyrian Orthodox parents
Atallah and Glades: one from the south of Syria, and one from the north
Charlie: Protestant leader in Beirut
Daoud: scholar from Sudan
Diane and Misho: Evangelical Christians from Syria
Emad: middle-class Egyptian pastor who has also lived in the West
Eva and Mohammad: poor, Kurdish, Sunni, Syrian refugees living in the Beirut area
Fou'ad: from a relatively wealthy family in Sudan
Karam: middle-class Protestant from Cairo

Lara: Jordanian Christian development worker among the desperately poor
Louisa: Druze professional from the Lebanese mountains, has lived on the Arabian Peninsula for several years
Marwan: middle-class, Maronite, Beiruti teen
Maryam: Muslim-background believer (MBB) from a privileged Yemeni clan
Maya and Ramy: from Homs
Nayla: Lebanese, lower-class, Orthodox woman divorced from a Muslim husband, attending a Protestant church
Nivin: from the Said in Egypt
Rabia: Orthodox Egyptian
Ram: Palestinian from a Muslim family
Rana: lower-middle-class teen, with a Shi'ite father and Sunni mother, originally from Syria, but living in Lebanon
Sayyid: Sunni Egyptian forced to work in a wealthier Middle Eastern country by economic necessity
Wade: lived eight years in Yemen (the only Westerner among the interviewees)
Zeina: Sunni, middle-class Beiruti, daughter of a sheikh

3

Righteousness, Wealth, and Teaching Morality to Children

Teaching Morality to Children

When my first interviewee, Ahmad, began to talk about child-rearing, I was uneasy. I began to wonder how I could get him back onto the topic of wealth and piety. It took a while for me to realize that, for Ahmad, child-rearing is a very important part of financial morality—perhaps *the* most important part.

Nearly all of my interviewees talked enthusiastically about how important upbringing is for formation in piety. They insisted that this, more than anything else, revealed the parents' actual standard of piety. Talking about attitudes of the wealthy toward the poor, Fou'ad from Sudan said:

> The family has a role. There are families which say, "God gave you everything you have: don't you dare be arrogant to others! Okay? Remember that once you were like them, at the same level. Don't you dare be arrogant toward them." There is a problem with some people. Maybe they don't have correct teaching in the home, or maybe they haven't grown in contentment, and just as soon as they get money, they get lofty, and they wear the best clothes, and that's the end: They see themselves better than all the other people. It's built on the teaching in the home.

Ram from Palestine agrees:

> Child-rearing is the most important point. How the family raises the son, what he hears from his family when he is little, [that's how] he grows. For this reason, in the families that bring in a lot of money, love money, think about money a lot, you will find a boy of six years thinking in the same way.

There was strong consensus that child-rearing practices are an important factor in determining the nature and extent of a person's economic morality in adulthood, and that failure to instill financial moral values in a child represents a moral failure on the part of the parent, and not merely an educational omission.

Child-rearing, Godliness, and Wealth

We go back to the first principle: upbringing. If he has been raised well and he has faith in God, he stays good.

For many, child-rearing is the determining factor in a person's standard of piety when it comes to wealth. In response to the question, "What is it that makes a person godly?" Zeina answered, "The first thing is his upbringing." Ahmad insisted, "The matter of riches doesn't make a person godly or evil. The evil and godliness go back to the environment in which the person was raised, and the upbringing with which he was brought up." Nearly all said that childhood training in material ethics will have a life-long effect. As Sayyid put it, "We go back to the first principle: upbringing. If he has been raised well and he has faith in God, he stays good."

Some Christian interviewees were explicit about their belief in the superiority of their religion for training children in financial ethics. For Elias, a Lebanese Maronite, an explicitly Christian upbringing is essential to prevent a person from falling into sin to get money: " . . . the most important thing for me as a Christian, and for my son Emile, is to learn the Christian religion. Because the Christian religion is the thing which prohibits these things that are happening . . . it is the Christian religion and the gospel which prohibit these things." Amjad from Iraq complained that Muslims raise their children in a schizophrenic manner, saying one thing about the pious use of money, but living differently. None of the Muslim interviewees made such a claim of superiority for Islam as the basis of training children in fiscal piety. I do not know whether this silence came from genuine respect for other traditions or from a reluctance to offend their Christian interviewer.

For Shi'ite Abu Nader, child-rearing is important because people are morally ignorant until someone tells them what is right and wrong. Parents should not assume that the child will naturally do what is right. On the contrary, they must teach the child everything. Abu Nader says, "But if I threw my son into the street and didn't teach him nor did I give him culture, and I didn't ask him, 'Where are you going, where are you coming [from]?' and it didn't matter to me if he learned or didn't learn, then he would become corrupted. Then I would come and hold him accountable. And he would respond, 'Okay, you didn't teach me!'" It is noteworthy that the training of his son[436] is the only concrete plan of action Abu Nader mentions in response to his long list of complaints about global evil.

The way parents raise their children has implications for the parents spiritually. Zeina says it most succinctly, "Child-rearing is the most important thing. *The* most important thing. God will hold us accountable if we have not raised our children well. For instance, 'What have you taught this child that he lies? Or steals?'" Some Muslims also saw a role for the believer in correcting others in society, "Guiding them on the correct path." Abu Nader gives this example, "If we see a person doing evil, we should censure him from it, distance him from it. And say to him, 'You're wrong.' If we see a person doing wrong, we should point out to him . . . If I see a person stealing, I will say, 'My uncle, don't steal!'"[437] Ahmad, also speaking

---

[436] Three of my interviewees each spoke primarily of training his or her son in monetary morality, although each of the three has daughters as well as a son. All of the single people who spoke hypothetically talked about raising sons.

[437] The term "my uncle" indicates that the person being rebuked is older than Abu Nader, a very socially awkward situation in the Middle East. I have heard other Muslims saying that verbal correction is necessary, even with people who are older, but should be done politely.

about verbal correction of the adult who steals, declares, "This one needs to be brought up," the same expression used throughout the interviews for child-rearing.

The closely knit family relationships which characterize the Middle East make moral training of children both easier and more necessary. Parents will be judged by the society for the way their children behave. Most of my interviewees have lived with or very near family as adults. It is common for parents to have adult children living with them, and some have plans for their children to live near them when they marry. Certainly this is the norm in Sudan and upper Egypt. Speaking of how her father-in-law invested in apartments so that his children could be near him, Zeina reflects, "He thought of his sons as his harvest . . . sons and daughters, I mean." Although urbanization and higher education are eroding the pattern, it is still not unusual for young adults to work with family members. Zeina remembers her family of origin fasting together and says:

> I am teaching them the correct way which I learned. I taught them prayer. And fasting. And they fasted when they were little . . . it is my duty to teach them these good things: honesty, how to get along with the world, and love people, and not to lie to anyone. And not make fun of anyone. I—this is the way my father raised me, and I want to raise my children this way. So that they do not do wrong.

All of the interviewers saw the close-knit family as a good thing, but Zeina again says it best, "I like it here, because in the future, when the children are big, there will be a house near here. Like their mother put them near herself—this is the way in Lebanon. This is how we like it."

Two of my interviewees also saw that the government and society in general have a *de facto* role in child-rearing, and believe that it is badly done. Louisa explained the vulnerability of Lebanese youth to temptation, "The way they are raised! Living in this country, no rules are followed, not even on the road." Karam from Egypt had a unique take on his government's corruption and economic mismanagement. He believed it taught blighted morality to young people:

> When there is no work, no money, when there is no good success, there is no teaching, all these factors have got to the point where the people are left lost. It's left the youth who are coming into the world killing themselves and they don't sense it. . . . Practically it is wrong. Foundationally wrong. Not wrong because he steals for food, but wrong because the economy of the country is wrong. The one who has a Bachelor's degree for 10 or 20 years is sitting [that is, doing nothing]. The one who has a doctorate is sitting. The one who has a diploma is sitting. So you see a youth who is like a rose going up to work at whatever work comes before him. He is going to decide between two things: either he is going to . . . migrate to another country to improve the level of his living and the living of his family, or he is going to walk like the world walks, and that's it. The corruption in Egypt is the result of "there isn't any." We've got to the level that those without money don't work and those with money don't work.

Economic Piety: What and How Do Families Teach?

Content

None of the interviewees set out to give a detailed and systematic curriculum for the training of children in the ethics of wealth, but between them, they provided an abundance of specifics. The general principles included love, respect for others, understanding, integrity, trustworthiness, using money as a means for good, the fear of God, earning money by hard work, honesty, staying out of debt, generosity, and contentment. These principles are passed down through the generations. Ahmad explained, "All that I am saying I have learned from my extended family, from my father and mother, because they raised us on these principles because the person who doesn't have values and principles isn't a human being."

Elias provided an extended example of the practical business wisdom that a son needs to learn from his father:

[My father] taught me a very important sentence. He asked me, "What is it in the rose that injures your hand? " I told him, "Thorns." He told me, "Write 'thorns' for me." So I wrote *shīn, wow, kāf* [the Arabic letters that spell "thorn"]. He told me, "If you want to live a [successful] life, I have experience. I have now lived 83 years, my son. And I want to give you this sentence, if you will remember it. *Shīn* means check. Don't ever, not once in your life, give someone a check without getting a receipt. *Wow*, don't be anyone's trustee. *Kāf*, don't be anyone's guarantor. And you will be at ease your whole life. Don't forget this, my son. "

Parents' Advice on Money and Morality
Here is a hodge-podge of advice taught by the interviewees' parents, or which they teach to their children:
- Take nothing that is not yours, not even an eraser you see lying on the floor.[438]
- Don't look into someone else's wallet, not even your father's.
- Know the value of money and that it comes through hard work.
- Money that comes from a source other than honest work goes quickly.
- Do not ask for financial help or borrow from anyone.
- "Whoever takes out a monkey [loan], the monkey stays and the money goes."
- When someone asks for help, you must give to them if you can.
- If you give, God will increase your money.
- If you pray, God will lift you out of financial trouble. If not, God will put you in the fire.
- Know what you can and cannot afford.
- Do not spend money for things you don't need.
- God gave you everything you have, so don't be arrogant.
- Learn how to manage money. Use money wisely.
- Go into trading, and be constantly improving your business.

---

[438] I heard the same advice, including the eraser, from interviewees from Sudan, Palestine, and Lebanon.

- Don't only work: You must give attention to your spiritual life.
- Save money: You don't know what will happen.
- Wage war on poverty; wage war on ignorance. Study is the key to future success.
- Money doesn't buy happiness.
- Observe all the rules of hospitality with every guest.

Methodology

Although I have used the term child-rearing for want of a better expression, most Middle Easterners assume that parental moral guidance is a lifelong obligation, and concentrated ethical teaching and oversight continue well into adulthood, as the "thorn" advice of Elie's father illustrates. Ahmad expressed dismay that Westerners abandon their children's moral education when they reach the age of 17, an observation I have regularly heard from Middle Easterners. In order to teach children proper values, parents need to be present in the home. Nayla voiced the concern I have heard expressed by many Lebanese that wealthy women are leaving the responsibility of rearing their children to foreign domestic workers in order to pursue selfish ends.

Most interviewees saw that the extended family augmented the family influence, especially when the children lived near or with the relatives. Rana explained:

> The extended family needs to know how to raise their children well and give freedom to the girl and the guy—the same thing. Because now we have got to a level, I'm telling you, the guys and the girls sit together so that wrong things happen. Why? No! Let your children stay under your eye. Let everything happen in front of you so that you know what right and wrong is happening. For example, if your son was getting drunk behind your back, or he is stealing or dealing, you're not going to know if he hasn't been with you. Let him stay with you and let him do what he wants, and he will see the wrong on his own.

However, despite very strong extended family nurture in some instances, the parents' influence on the moral development of the child was generally seen as paramount.

Beyond the parents and the extended family, the school and the church or mosque may have some influence on the development of the moral values of a person. The degree of this influence varied according to the country and individual. The Syrians I heard from were particularly positive about the role of schools and communities of worship in moral formation, but they were the exception. Most others saw school as a minor adjunct to the primary ethical instruction of the home. All saw the role of the mosque or the church in teaching children piety as secondary at best. The strong majority of those I interviewed are devout in their religious persuasion and practice, so silence on the subject of religious institutional moral training is not based on ignorance of what is offered. Not one parent expressed any expectation that their children would learn right attitudes and behaviors toward money from the mosque, church, Druze gathering, or school. Marwan, a high school student, explained why religion has little effect on financial piety: "There is no effect because, for example, can someone from church tell you, 'Spend here and don't spend there'? They do guidance sessions about drugs and that sort of thing, but . . . no." Home was far more significant to moral development than the programs and influence of extra-familial religious institutions. The two youngest of my interviewees mentioned also the importance of friends in influencing moral choices, either for good or ill.

Not all moral teaching at home would meet with the approval of most Westerners. Take the approach of Rana's family, for example:

> There are people you have to frighten for them to pray. God, if you don't pray, will put you in the fire, or if you lie, God sees you and will come and strangle you in the night. This is what they told us when we were little. And until today. Now my sister's little son, in order to draw him closer to God, we say this sort of thing to him. God will come to the unbelievers and strangle us, kill us. So the boy will have fear, and will turn out content with God.

Children learn more about the principles and specific requirements of material piety from their parents' lives than from their words. Parental example was held up as the primary method of passing on to the next generation piety with regard to wealth. Elias tells this story about his father:

> He had a hotel, and a priest would come and say, 'Mr. M., we are in need of . . . because there are now many poor due to the war.' And my father would call me and tell me, 'In circumstances like this, as long as God (May he be praised and exalted) gives to us, I want you to come and learn from me. Stretch out your hand to the poor. Give, but what your right hand does, your left hand must not know about it. I mean extremely secret—between you and the priest.'

There was a strong consensus that parents cannot teach their children proper financial morality unless they provide adequately for them, but not lavishly. Zeina says, for example:

> I am not stingy with my children. I need to give to them. I need to teach them the very best knowledge. I get them good clothes. . . . In this way one teaches his children how to live. They grow up knowing what they want. They don't look at other people, "Look what he's wearing." No!

Eva agreed and knew from experience that this is possible, even on a small salary. She recalled, "My father was a [blue collar] worker in Syria. That means he had a very small salary. All our lives we never went without, and he never made us feel as though we didn't have money. Everything was in our hands, and not one day did we sense that a worker lived among us." Louisa remembered, "What did my parents teach me about money? Formal teaching, no. But we grew up in a house where they tried to provide us with all that we needed, for education, for dresses, for everything." Several interviewees talked about failure to meet the financial needs of the family as a cause of lack of piety in the children.

Providing for needs is one thing, but Louisa warned against spoiling children:

> You see children living like adults. They are not living their age. You don't see children playing like we used to. We have a nice area, a pleasant, clean environment. Afternoons we would come home and, after we finished our studies, we used to play. Now, if you walk through a whole village you can barely see one child playing outside. Either they are on their iPads or tablets or . . . I think many things were not provided for people when they were young, and they want to provide them for their children, not to withhold from them. But I believe in raising up children. If you believe you were raised up in the proper way, then preserve the culture, the mentality. Now nothing means anything to children, unfortunately. Nothing. You give him a prize. It used to be that a child couldn't sleep if they get this prize. Now, it means nothing. A gift? Every day they are getting gifts!

The righteous rich in the Middle East are devout mothers and fathers who consciously work to pass on high moral values to their children by teaching and example. They are aware that the way they bring up their child has lasting implications for the child, the parents (who must answer to God), and the society. In addition to moral wisdom, the parents will provide guidance in economic practicalities.

Middle Eastern Child-rearing, Wealth, Righteousness, and the Bible

The issue of child-rearing is one in which Middle Eastern society is much closer to biblical teaching than Western society. The importance of training one's children in piety is taught in the books of Deuteronomy, Job, Proverbs, and 1 Timothy, among others. The Bible contains many examples, commands, and exhortations which resonate with themes mentioned above:

- the family as the primary agent of moral instruction
- parental teaching and moral guidance extending into adulthood

- integrating economic ethics and good fiscal advice into general moral and religious nurture
- teaching through intentional instruction, daily guidance, and example
- the credibility of the parent resting at least in part on the moral performance of the children
- the responsibility of both parents to teach their children right and wrong with the support of extended family

The Bible, like Middle Eastern culture, recognizes the general principle that people will mature according to their upbringing. However, the Scriptures tend to be less deterministic than most of my interviewees, recognizing, on the one hand, that children can reject their godly heritage and, on the other, rejoicing in the power of God to transform people steeped in sin.

It is dangerous to make a case from silence. However, two theological gaps yawn dangerously; gaps which regional experiences tell me reveal foundational problems. The first is the lack of admission by any of the interviewees who talked extensively about child-rearing that they or their children are incapable of living up to God's standards, and therefore are in need of grace. Most seem convinced that correct teaching and guidance from family and associates will be sufficient to produce a pious son or daughter. Ahmad calls weak those who envy, gossip, are stingy, or steal, but offers no solution stronger than *tarbiya*—upbringing.[439] In fact, there was little acknowledgment of a problem, at least as far as the interviewees and their families are concerned. Regional culture would preclude the baring of a personal or family flaw, especially in a taped interview, but there was no hint, even in theory, of human moral inadequacy which cannot be overcome by human means, except in an affirmation by Nayla that what makes a person godly is the Father's erasing of the registration of sin, and in her testimony of God's transforming power in her life when she was at rock bottom.

The second gap in theology follows logically from the first: I wonder about the apparent confidence of the interviewees that they

---

[439] Obviously Ahmad has in mind here guidance given by others in society to an adult, but his word choice is interesting.

are godly people and able to train their children in righteousness through instruction and behavior modification. God seems rather passive in the process.

Teaching Children Morality in Practice

Western parents living in the Middle East can learn a great deal about wholesome child-rearing practices from their adopted environment. Parents will find they enjoy the support of society in their efforts to teach morality. The cost of that support is putting up with unsolicited advice from others. Westerners serving in the Middle East who find the intrusion of others into their child-rearing practices would do well to ask locals how they handle such situations.[440]

...there was no hint, even in theory, of human moral inadequacy which cannot be overcome by human means.

Cross-cultural workers who are parents should consider seriously how they are training their children in godliness. They need a plan, agreed upon by both parents where possible, that involves providing the child with principles, biblical bases, daily guidance, accountability, and especially, example. Parents should consider all that a fully mature adult needs to know about earning, saving, spending, using, giving, investing, guarding, and bequeathing money. Lifestyle choices also need to be contemplated, and how to face money related temptations. This wisdom can be taught and reinforced through a variety of methods over the course of the parents' lifetime. Parents who must be separated from their children when they are teenagers or young adults should seek to maintain positive influence and a level of accountability on the children through correspondence and the nurture of trusted friends and relations. This is not only imperative for the glory of God, the well-being of the family, and the spiritual good of the children, but may prove essential for gaining respect and a hearing in Middle Eastern society.

---

[440] Greg Livingstone recommends the same is his book *Planting Churches in Muslim Cities: A Team Approach* (Grand Rapids: Baker, 1993), 129–130.

Mothers in ministry need to be particularly careful that they are neither neglecting their children nor being perceived as doing so. The visits the personal evangelist considers an essential part of her work may seem to her Middle Eastern neighbors an exercise in self-indulgence if her children are ignored, cared for by non-family members, or regularly fed quick foods of questionable nutritional value. The Bible contains more injunctions to fathers about child-rearing than to mothers, and fathers who value the Scriptures and the calling and gifts of their wives will ensure that they also devote themselves to the upbringing of their sons and daughters.

Middle Eastern parents believe in the importance of a wise and pious up-bringing, but that doesn't mean that everyone knows how to do it well. In Yemen, for example, few parents teach their children long-term financial planning, and many would be unable to do so because they themselves have never been taught. Middle Eastern societies in general take less offense at *tadakhkhul*, butting in, than Western societies do, and with sensitivity and tact one may be able to offer advice to parents. But care needs to be taken lest a criticism of the behavior of the child be perceived as impugning the honor of the family.

Informal discussions on the subject of teaching children about wealth and piety could be a relatively upbeat and non-threatening way to raise spiritual issues with Middle Easterners of any background. Since this is an area in which there are many shared values, it could serve as a bridge with the many parents who are genuinely seeking godliness for themselves and their progeny. Middle Easterners of all denominations are open to learn from the lives and teachings of the prophets on moral issues, and distinctly biblical ideas can be introduced into a conversation about child-rearing by telling stories of the prophets or reading their teachings. For Muslims in particular, religion and law are virtually synonymous. Sometimes it is necessary to display a grasp of divine wisdom about practical ethics before one has the credibility to talk doctrine. Ethics and child-rearing are a good starting point for witness, provided it is a humble witness.

My experience is that individual workers, churches, and particularly schools may find surprisingly strong support from parents for ethics programs, even from people of very different denominational backgrounds. Arabs do not believe in a morally neutral curriculum. However, the relative quiet about such programs in the interviews suggests a need for honest evaluation of the results of such programs. Unless the parents affirm and exemplify what is taught outside the home, the impact is likely to be limited. Nonetheless, ethics programs can have profound effects on individuals, and can be a constructive means for building relationships, establishing valuable dialogue, and helping families.

4

Praising God and Acknowledging His Sovereignty

One of the most striking features for a Western reader of the interview transcripts is the frequency with which God is mentioned. While the religious nature of the topic invites comment about God, most of the interviewees peppered their speech liberally with eruptions of praise, thanks, and confidence in God. No Middle Easterner would find this way of speaking at all extraordinary: it is characteristic throughout the Arab world. These expressions are a matter of course. And Arabs are proud of it: Syrians, Sudanese, Egyptians and Yemenis bragged to me that they say these things more often even than do the Lebanese. Rabi' from Egypt says, "When someone asks you your news—like 'How is your health?'—the first thing that comes to your mind is, 'May the goodness of God increase!' or 'Praise God!'" Although there are many such phrases, the most common phrases of this type are "praise God" *al-ḥamdu lillāh*, "The livelihood is from God" *ar-rizq min Allah,* and "The ownership is God's" *al-mulk lillāh*. Muslims often remind one another, "Don't forget to mention God!" and say, "Praised and Exalted" *subḥān wata' āla* after referring to God, even mid-sentence. Such sayings are constantly on the lips of the pious person.

These expressions of God's acclaim and reign reveal the interviewees' theology of God and money. All of the interviewees believe ardently that God is the ultimate source of material prosperity. God is the source even when there is also an obvious natural or social explanation for a boon, such as a friend bringing a food basket. I asked Zeina, "What is the role of God in the economic situation?" and she answered, "Everything! God is the one who gives people their living. This is very important, to know that the money is something God sends. If God had not helped us and stood by us, then we would be nothing." Elias learned a daily ritual to remind him that God is the provider:

> Every morning my father would teach me to say, "O Opening, O Livelihood. O Opening, O Livelihood." This means that God gives the livelihood. Whenever we start some new work, we begin either by prayer or by saying this phrase, "May God prosper us." And God gives the livelihood. *God* gives the livelihood.

Since God is the one who provides, he deserves the praise and thanks. I gave up counting the times the interviewees give God thanks and praise for their good economic situations.

Interviewees did not hesitate to ascribe their bad fortune to God any more than they did to ascribe their good fortune to him. Referring to an unhappy situation, Ahmad stated outright, "God put me in that house for four years." But interviewees also made it clear that God should be praised in all circumstances, whether good, bad, or doubtful. If hard times fall within God's sovereignty, the correct response is not to address him with blame and anger. Zeina said, "If you get $1000, you say, 'Praise God.' Maybe next time, what comes to me is $2. I say 'Praise God' again." One survey respondent described a good man: "No matter what financial or health problems face him, he says, 'Praise God. Nothing happens to us except what God wills.'" The interviewees gave God thanks and praise for (or in spite of) their economic reversals, sometimes in surprising ways. When describing his devastating financial situation, Ahmad ended his answer with, "Praise God, Lord of the Worlds." Nayla's response was similar: "Thank God, I am content. Thank God, my current situation is not comfortable." Elias said, "I can thank my Lord that later we were tried and went down monetarily." Abu Nader spoke frankly about how small his house is and how his two adult daughters and a teenage son share one room, and concluded, "We aren't able to do better than that. Praise God."

The central idea of Islam is submission to the will of God, an important idea also in Christian thought. Therefore, it is not surprising to find in ordinary conversations frequent expressions of resignation to the will of God and to the circumstances which he has ordained. One constantly hears them at funerals: "It was the will of God," or "God wrote it this way." Accepting God's will means contentment, freedom from envy, and a willingness to be humbled.

Some have questioned the genuineness of these habitual laudations. I have on several occasions heard people in distress tack "praise God" onto their complaint in funereal tones. A Sudanese student wondered aloud, "To what degree do the people comprehend when they say, 'praise God'? It's just a word that is said. But if you talk with the person, they will curse violently the situation of the country; they will curse the poverty." But his companion, also from Sudan, protested that this is a small minority of the people: the majority adore God's generosity.

The wording of these pious sayings sometimes functions as a religious boundary marker, most notably when Protestants substitute "We thank God," *nashkur Allah* for "Praise to God." Iraqi Pastor Amjad viewed the Muslim version as sometimes heartfelt gratitude, but more often as an empty platitude uttered for show. He believed Protestants say "We thank God" as an expression of sincere faith, and I have heard similar opinions expressed by Protestants throughout the region. Lebanese Pastor Charlie also considered the practice of frequently quoting these sayings Islamic in origin and often hypocritical:

> They would put a sign on the building, "The ownership is God's," *al-mulk lillāh*, but the subliminal message is "The rental is for the owner of the building." It might say, "The ownership is God's," but that's where God ends: on the sign. It's just for show. There's really no real gratitude. Again, there are always exceptions.

Palestinian MBB Ram was also disturbed by hypocrisy in the use of these pious phrases: "'The ownership is God's.' Yeah. You hear the talk, but I don't sense that there is much thanks."

Ramy from Syria took a positive angle: "There are sayings in Islam which help them succeed [in giving secretly]. The most important is, 'The ownership is God's,' for the Muslim doesn't believe he owns anything. He says to you about everything, 'The ownership is God's.'"

The relationship between God's sovereignty and human responsibility came up frequently. Faith in the sovereignty and provision of God does not deny, in the minds of the interviewees, the role of human individuals and systems in determining economic well-being. Zeina explains:

> [God] provides the livelihood, if you are sensible with your money. You mustn't spend it all. You must hide a bit, leave a bit for emergencies, for necessities. You can't spend it all just like that—it's gone. No. You've got to think about the future. Perhaps you'll be squeezed, or something will happen. And God helps a lot.

Marwan complained of his classmates at exam time, "They say, 'O Lord, make us succeed, make us succeed, make us succeed,' even though they haven't studied in order to succeed. How will he make you succeed?! By what means?!"

Fou'ad took objection to what he felt were false promises made in God's name. He said:

> Everyone exerts himself to get money. I have confidence that God will open doors for you to work and get money by your effort. Okay, he will support you, help you, open ways before you that you can't imagine. But there are people who think if they give, God will pour money on them. Maybe instead he will open ways for you to come up with money.

One can hear Abu Nader's struggle to maintain both faith in God as provider and realism about the human role in economics in the following dialogue:

Abu Nader: What I want is to educate my children, and get them proper medical treatment: take them to the doctor. Okay? I want in the future, when I am 60 or 65 years old, that they can feed me. Who is going to feed me? Who?
Umm Nader: Your son.
Abu Nader: Okay, tomorrow, let's say that my son isn't able to find employment. Who is going to feed me? This is a problem. So I must depend upon God. God is the one who will make me able. But who will feed me I don't know.
Karen: God is able to do anything.
Abu Nader: Okay, God is able to do anything, but we have to work in the end, don't we?

Amjad noted that many Iraqis optimistically quote the saying, "Spend what is in the pocket: He [God] gives what is absent." That is, God provides when we've run out.

A heated discussion broke out during my interview of a group of Egyptians regarding the relationship between the providence of God and family planning. Some asserted that these expressions of praise and confidence in the provision of God were being misused to promote fatalism and perpetuate poverty. Coptic Orthodox Rabi' argued, "There is not a lot of benefit in producing fifteen children when there is no money, and then saying, 'The livelihood!' That's not right—ever!" Sunni Sayyid responded:

> I do not agree because God created the sons of Adam with whatever was to be. Maybe, for instance, he doesn't have money. Maybe he will be a millionaire. This, may God be praised and exalted, is how he makes the sons of Adam. He is the one who gives him the living. So you had a son. You go back and have another son—or another daughter. Doesn't the second daughter come with a livelihood? She comes with a livelihood. God, may he be praised and exalted, foreordained it. Isn't that right? Any person among us, from the time he began in his mother's womb, God wrote for him, about him. God wrote his livelihood. He wrote everything in his life. He wrote when he would die.

This is an ongoing debate in Egypt, with the poor, the rural population and the Muslims more often emphasizing God's sovereign providence, and the educated, the urbanites, and the Christians tending to major on human responsibility. One side accuses the other of irresponsibility and in return gets an earful about lack of genuine trust in God. The debate is certainly not unique to Egypt in the region.

Of course, no one gave a systematic explanation of the relationship between God's immutable will and human choice, but some of the interviewees made note of specific ways in which God responds to human choices. Ahmad's wife, Alia, liked an Islamic proverb which suggests that offering thanks launches a spiral of bounty and praise: "If you thank Me, I'll give you more." In answer to my question about her children's future, Zeina said:

> If it is God's will, O God! I educate them well so that, if God wills, they will work well and will be good in society. And if God wills, it will be as God has written for them. I figure that if I have raised them well, God willing, they will turn out well.

Several of the interviewees believed in a correlation between piety and material blessing, among them the Lebanese Sunni Zeina: "Money, if it is going along with piety, is acceptable money, and God blesses it." Eva, a Kurdish Syrian, warned about the consequence of forgetting God: "If you knocked on God's door after having forgotten him, he won't answer." Coptic Orthodox Rabi' quoted Malachi,[441] "God says, 'Test me in this.'" Based on what she had learned at school, Rana, a Syrian Shi'ite, told me, "When you are praying, God is watching you, and he will lift you out of this problem with the least damage." But, she saw this as a generalization rather than a hard-and-fast rule, for she added, "Now is the fast of Ramadan. But even though I am praying, this same [bad] thing is happening to me. God is testing us. Even if it happens like this, don't go to the wrong!"

Not everyone held that human actions and attitude determine divine bestowals. Sayyid, while vehemently insisting on God's

---

[441] Malachi 3:10.

absolute sovereignty, with equal vehemence insisted that God's choice for a person's fate is totally unrelated to whether the person has faith. Rana also believed that God doesn't necessarily give the believer money, but "tests him, so that he will stay near to him."

People in the Arab world often adhere to the concept of divine compensation for poverty and loss. Zeina thought that God repays a person who uses his money to help others, although perhaps the repayment might not be monetary, but in some other area of life, such as good health. Elias hoped aloud that God would compensate him for his troubles in four ways. First, he was confident that, when God wills that a person suffer, he gives courage and power to the sufferer. Second, he was certain that difficult circumstances are meant for his good:

> God loves me and he taught me to be in the middle class and to feel with the poor . . . And God (may he be praised and exalted) taught me that I should be humble, and get what is needed, not to live in an artificial way.

He expanded on the reason behind his losses:

> So that I can learn about money. Before, I wasn't like I am now—humble, and I feel with the poor and the unemployed, and such like. Maybe this is from God so that I can understand the value of wealth.

Third, Elias anticipated that, one day, God would restore his former wealth. He said, "I think I may lose some of what I spent, but God will return it," and "If God closes off a place, he opens another." One Druze and two Muslim interviewees shared a variation of this thought, that if God takes away in one area of life, he sends compensatory blessings in another. Finally, Elias hoped that there might be some eternal compensation: " . . . maybe God will receive us in heaven because we went through this hell on earth."

Rabi' was concerned that a belief in material rewards for piety could lead to people doing good with a profit motive. He protested,

"We do for heaven, and not for earth. Your piety is for God: your prayers, your tithes, your *zakat*, these are for our Lord, not for the slave. Poverty or wealth don't come into it at all."

Whatever role the individual may have in influencing his or her future, my interviewees were in complete agreement, 1) that God is ultimately in control and he determines people's fortunes, and 2) that he is worthy of praise in all circumstances. The person who fears God will praise him frequently without regard to the vicissitudes through which that person passes.

All the interviewees who spoke to me in Arabic modeled what they believe about praising God and acquiescing to his will.[442] In so doing, they expressed how they, and many Middle Easterners like them, expect a righteous person to speak, regardless of his or her economic status or the ups and downs of life. Pious people praise God publicly and continually, in bad times as well as in good, as an affirmation that they are content with what God has chosen for them. They recognize his control over their fates, and submit to his will with gratitude.[443] They prefix their plans with the phrase, "If God wills . . . ," but do not use the will of God as an excuse for inaction or self-indulgence. A godly rich person will be characterized by contentment, acclaim for God, and humble, patient acceptance of setbacks.

---

[442] Interestingly, the English interviews have few of these sparks of praise, and I noticed myself and others who know both languages unconsciously increasing or reducing the frequency according to the language.

[443] Part of this is due to two Muslim emphases. The first, an almost unrelieved stress on predestination, is theological. The second is more practical, and can be summed up in the oft repeated phrase, "Don't forget the mention of (dhikr) God." The practice of mentioning or remembering God (and particularly the Arabic word Allah attributed to him as his name), also finds expression in countless daily informal prayers, oaths, and blessings. See Raphael Patai, *The Arab Mind*, (New York: Scribner's, 1973), 147–150.

Piety and Class

There was a considerable range of opinion about the relationship between class and piety, between the amount of wealth with which people are blessed and their moral health. A number claimed it made no difference, but then almost immediately explained why each class relates to God and temptation differently. What follows is a selection of their views.

- "Great wealth is evidence, not of God's blessing, but of ungodly behavior." (lower-class Lebanese Shi'ite and lower-class Lebanese Christian)
- "Pride in money is the greatest temptation." (Sudanese)
- "Sometimes the poor person considers that he is hard done by, and maybe that God is the One who wronged him." (Lebanese middle-class Sunni)
- "The middle class is more inclined to piety, because he is neither rich nor poor. The rich says, 'I have everything. Why should I go toward piety? Why should I take refuge in God?' The middle class doesn't have a lot that keeps him from piety, but also he isn't poor enough to say, 'God doesn't love me, he doesn't give to me.'" She changed her mind a minute later. "The poor person is constantly crying out to God, and depends on God." (Syrian refugee from a middle-class family.)
- "The poor, I find, are closest to their Lord, but when they become rich they forget. They come to run after money. Very few of them, if they become wealthier, continue walking in what is right. The poor are always looking to God to help them. Then there are some who, when their situation improves, stay with God . . . it depends. Some forget who it is that is giving to them." (middle-class Lebanese)
- "You find people who are poor and pious, but to appear so in the eyes of the people is very difficult. It's hard for the poor to appear positively. Very, very difficult. If there isn't a lot of personal benefit in this person, it is hard to show him respect." (Palestinian)

- "The person whose material circumstances are better, and who has more work, will be busy. And because he is busy, he will be tied more to his business and his material life, more than he is tied to our Lord." (Egyptian middle-class)
- "If one has a lot of money, he leaves our Lord—that's it! That's it. 'I don't want to pray; I don't want to go to the church, I don't want to go to the mosque. I am satisfied. God has given me all I possess,'—so he leaves. There is no more piety. He follows his own desires." (Upper Egyptian, middle-class Coptic evangelical)
- "Whether you have money or not, you need to have strength of will to be a believer. The rich who are not pious let money drive them, and the poor who are not pious don't believe God is able to meet their needs." (mixed Syrian/Lebanese, Shi'ite/Sunni)
- "Most people whose money increases become distant. They have less piety. The person who walks in piety doesn't have a lot of money, and it is hard for him to come to have money." (Palestinian)
- "The very religious person who had no money but came to have some is going to pay attention to what happened and keep believing. But the one who was born with money, what does he want? 'I have money. I have everything. I'm not going to get closer [to] or entrust God with my life.'" (middle-class Lebanese Maronite)
- "It should be a plus if you have money and you're religious in that, if you are wise, you use the money to help others. This is part of our religion." (Lebanese Druze)

Praise, Sovereignty, and the Bible

Once again, the Middle Easterners have got it mostly right. In honoring God as the Creator and Provider, my interviewees reflect the mood and teaching of the Scriptures, particularly the Psalms and the Pauline letters. Also biblical, and especially in keeping with Deuteronomy, is their belief that their material well-being depends on the will and the blessing of God. They faithfully abide by the injunction in James' epistle to avoid boasting by verbalizing the sovereignty of God's will. Like the Scriptures, particularly the Proverbs and Paul, most believe human responsibility and choice to have real consequences for the economic well-being of the individual or family. With Job, they are determined to show their gratitude to God in all circumstances, even the most trying. The interviews reminded me of 1 Thessalonians 5:18, "Give thanks in all circumstances, for this is God's will for you . . ."[444] The interviewees were unanimous in supporting the teaching of God's word that the blessing of God comes in many forms, and money is only one of them, and not the most important. And like the Deuteronomist, they have no intention of letting themselves or others forget what God has done for them.

Yet again, my concerns largely take the form of omissions. Middle Eastern Christians and Muslims both use the term *Allah* in referring to the One God, but of course, the Muslims would not include in that Divine Oneness him through whom "all things were made; without him nothing was made that has been made."[445] Christ's role as Creator and Provider is probably assumed by the Christians interviewed, but they make no mention of it. Elias looks to the saints, and particularly to Mary, as a source of protection and answered prayer.

God's right to rule according to his will was rightly defended by all of the interviewees, but I miss among the Muslims the sense of God's tender care as a loving Father which Jesus so passionately believed and taught. I also miss in all of the interviews the place found in the Scriptures, and particularly the Psalms, for the faithful to cry out to God in honest complaint and lament.[446]

Both Islam and Christianity in the region play host to some questionable teachings about piety guaranteeing prosperity, or human actions determining divine responses. While these are not

---

[444] The omission of the phrase "in Christ Jesus" is significant. See the next paragraph.
[445] John 1:3. See also 1 Corinthians 8:6; Colossians 1:16; Hebrews 1:2.
[446] Kenneth Cragg articulates this concern powerfully in his article, "The Riddle of Man and the Silence of God: A Christian Perception of Muslim Response" (*International Bulletin of Missionary Research*, vol. 17, #4, October 1993, 160–163).

the official teachings, they enjoy widespread popularity and present a threat to genuine trust in God and recognition of his sovereignty.

It is good to praise God continually.[447] However, anything done continually can become mindlessly habitual, including exclamations of praise and submission, like "May he be praised and exalted!" or "If God wills. . . ." As a believer who grew up in the secular West, I found these brief expressions of piety refreshing at first, and I still often do. But sometimes I wonder if we really think about the one we honor with our lips. A comparable phenomenon in the West might be saying, "God bless you!" after a sneeze. While I would not for a moment discourage anyone from using these true and worthy exclamations, the Scriptures make clear that we should speak sincerely, ensuring that our words are more than empty ritual or an empty show of piety.

Praise and God's Sovereignty in Practice

In the West, only a religious kook answers, "Praise God!" to questions like, "How are you?" "Did you have enough to eat?" "Are you married?" "What is your salary?" And *nobody* says, "The doctor tells me I have inoperable cancer, thank God." In the Middle East, most people speak this way, regardless of their religious tradition. Expatriates who rarely acknowledge God's greatness and lordship with their lips cannot expect Middle Easterners to take them seriously as pious people.

Likewise, in keeping with James 4:13–17, missionaries should frequently remind themselves and others that all plans for the future are subject to the will of God. If stock phrases used by Middle Easterners seem artificial and overused to the point of meaninglessness, it's usually safe, and often edifying, to personalize them slightly. For example, one might say, "Praise God! He really is generous, isn't he?" Or one might opt for greater transparency than is normal: "I'm finding it very hard to praise God today, and yet I know he is great and worthy of praise." It would also be well to keep anguished cries of, "Why, God?" for personal prayer and perhaps a few trusted, believing friends.

---

[447] Psalm 34:1.

In addition to being offensive, complaints about Middle Eastern culture convey to the local people that the complainer is not content with the lot God has given him or her. Grumbling about how much things cost or how little one has smacks of ingratitude to God, and neither God nor those around really want to hear it. This is especially true when the person complaining seems to the listeners to be better off than they are. Zeina's echo of Moses[448] is worth repeating: "the rich person cannot be righteous unless he or she remembers gratefully whence the money comes." Self-examination is in order:

> Grumbling about how much things cost or how little one has smacks of ingratitude to God, and neither God nor those around really want to hear it. This is especially true when the person complaining seems to the listeners to be better off than they are.

- Do I habitually see God as the source of my finances, health, successes, and the many blessings of my life?
- Am I a thoroughly grateful person in word and attitude?
- Does my admiration of God bubble forth just as exuberantly in times of trouble as in times of relative ease?

Daily life in the Middle East abounds with opportunities to discuss with people the relationship between divine sovereignty and human responsibility. These questions are rarely asked for purely academic reasons. They may represent personal anguish or fear, a sense of hopelessness, a loss of faith, or an attempt at cultural or religious imperialism. Therefore, answers need to be pastorally sensitive as well as biblically and theologically sound.

Expatriates are wise to be cautious about assuming the superiority of their own ideas regarding divine sovereignty and human initiatives in daily matters. There are three reasons for this. I will illustrate using the subject of birth control, since it is one of the matters hotly debated in the region. First, Western values are not necessarily biblical values. As comfortable as I am personally with birth control, I recognize that the Bible speaks of the abundance of children as a

---

[448] Deuteronomy 8.

blessing from God, and that many wise and godly people around the world differ with me. Second, we don't always fully understand the implications of our favored practices for another culture. For example, children are the surest form of security in old age for most Middle Easterners, child mortality rates are higher in the rural Middle East than in the West, the high emigration rate is leaving many elderly people abandoned in countries without suitable institutions to care for them, and many people value family and clan cohesion more highly than personal advancement. On more than one occasion, I have heard Westerners advocating to Arab Christians for both birth control and democratic government in one breath without having considered the long-term political implications of this combination for a precariously placed minority. Third, unless we express ourselves very precisely (in Arabic!), we may give the impression that we don't believe in the providence of God, and that our wealth has caused us to rely on ourselves rather than on God, the source of all things. That seems to be the impression Sayyid was getting of Christians during the debate among the Egyptian interviewees.

It is common in discussions among new Western workers to express frustration with the question, "Where does your money come from?" I will discuss in a later chapter the difficulties one faces in either avoiding answering or answering frankly, but *accompanying* the answer one gives should be a grateful acknowledgment that the worker's income is ultimately from God. *Al-ḥamdu-lillāh!*

5

Generosity

I'm no detective, but it didn't take me long to figure out the basic plot. The gifts of food from a neighbor were the first clue. Then followed a host of other clues: the incessant invitations to visits and meals, watching friends at restaurants fight to get the bill first, a poor taxi driver refusing to take a fare from a new arrival to his country, the popularity of the name "Karim" and its variations[449]—all these and more alerted me to the fact that generosity is one of the core values of Middle Eastern society.

For several I interviewed, generosity is the essence of piety. Maryam used the two terms synonymously. Karam said, "What identifies the pious person specifically is his willingness to give." Nivin distinguished between a good and a bad person on the basis of whether "he is pious or he keeps the thing that God has given him." Sabt, a Christian, said, "If I have money in my pocket, I don't know Christ." The righteous rich person, first and foremost, will be a person who, as Nivin put it, "loves to be generous," or to use Charlie's words, gives " . . . with a joyful heart, giving all that you can give because you love the Lord." Some Syrians, explaining the importance of openhandedness, claimed that in their country even an atheist who gives will be considered pious by many.[450] Generosity is an attitude of grace which results in habitual, voluntary giving. This giving takes a variety of forms.

---

[449] The name means "generous" and it is a close cognate of one of the primary words for "honor."
[450] However, Louise strongly disagreed with the idea that atheists could be pious.

> **A Dissenting View**
> Unlike most of the others I talked to, Charlie didn't put much stock in the generosity of his culture. Discussing with me the current economic problems in Lebanon, he said, after having acknowledged political and economic factors:
>
> Here's the biggest issue that people don't see, which basically shows up in all the other things I've mentioned: selfishness! People tend to be grabby. It's a selfish country. It shows up in the way we drive, the way we give or don't give. Even when we give, a lot of the time we are giving for selfish reasons. It shows up in our spending priorities and trends. An economy built on selfishness will crumble.

Giving to God

A few of the interviewees—Christians in particular—mentioned giving to God through tithes and offering as an act of worship distinct from giving to the poor or hospitality. Muslims distinguished between paying the *zakat*, helping the poor, and giving as a means of gaining atonement, but in every case, whether building a mosque or giving a beggar a sandwich, each act was seen as giving to God. Zeina recommends the prayer, "O Lord, to you. This money that I give to the poor is for you."

Generosity to Family

When asked to describe what *bad*, rich people are like, Muhammad focused on the home: "Even in their house they are not good. Stingy. They are rich and there is nothing in their house and they deny their children everything." His wife, Eva agreed, characterizing the pious rich person as one whose generosity begins at home. She said, "He opens his hand to his wife and children. He doesn't say no to anything. He says no to himself, but not to his children." After Maryam's father died and left his wife and children without an income, the extended family came daily to the house to make sure their needs were met, as is the duty of relatives: "There is always this expectation that we offer support to the needy in the family."

Sometimes this generosity can be costly indeed. A friend of ours in Syria went to work for two years in Libya in order to earn enough for the furnished apartment he would need to get married. He hated his life there, but stuck at it because he knew it was the only way he would be able to afford to marry. Shortly before he was to return, his sister became ill and needed expensive treatment. He did what was expected of him, and paid for the treatment, thereby gutting the large sum he had saved. He never married.

Hospitality

There are few biblical injunctions which Arabs of all stripes practice with more relish than these: "Practice hospitality," "Do not forget to entertain strangers," and "Outdo one another in showing honor."[451] For Maryam from Yemen, hospitality was foundational to piety and essential to preserving an honorable identity. Throughout the Middle East, and particularly in the countryside, it is not uncommon for a person to be verbally lassoed or even physically cajoled into a home for a visit and virtually force fed homemade desserts and sweet tea. Hosts and hostesses seem to take a perverse pleasure in compelling guests to distend their stomachs to unnatural proportions. People even go into debt to conform to the obligation of hospitality, from the very poor person who borrows sugar from a neighbor to serve guests tea, to the tycoon's son who begins his married life with a bank loan for tens of thousands of dollars because he feels obligated to honor his wedding guests. Arabs are appalled at the "shameful"[452] but common Western practice of splitting the restaurant tab between friends. They are more likely to fight one another for the privilege of paying. First-time visitors to one's home, city, or country must be given a nearly royal reception and not allowed to pay for anything. I told some Egyptians about being outsmarted by one of their countrymen who arrived at the restaurant substantially ahead of our appointment and paid in advance to guarantee that he would

---

[451] Romans 12:13; Hebrews 13:2; and Romans 12:10 (ESV).
[452] To quote Karam and many others I have heard.

get to pay. The group nodded with proud satisfaction, and one said, "You weren't able to laugh at his expense."

Helping the Poor

For all of the interviewees, aiding the poor was essential to piety. Not one of them doubted the greatness of the need or the goodness of the deed. They praised both systematic, proportional giving and spontaneous giving. An open heart is the goal, and not merely an open wallet. Pastor Charlie explained what he wanted his congregation to know about wealth and piety:

> A very important lesson is to be a giving people. Amounts don't matter, but rather attitudes. If I'm able to give $10, what's $10? It's almost nothing in the scheme of things. But I'm going to give it anyway because that's how much I can, and I want to. It's the wanting to give rather than the gift itself.

Charlie believed that giving is not a strong cultural trait in the region, regardless of the theoretical acclaim people give to it. Marwan was inclined to agree. He said, "Now religion tells you to give to the poor, collect for the poor, but it doesn't have much effect. On the contrary, money affects religion. This is the reality, but few people admit that it is so."

Giving is essential to piety because God is generous. Official Islamic doctrine doesn't think in terms of "communicable attributes of God," but beggars call out "God is generous," and the implication is that the passerby should be as well. For the Christians, God's magnanimity was foundational to human generosity. Nayla believed that one of the reasons God gives to us is so that we can help others. Drawing on Scripture, she pointed out that giving isn't all that costly: "The rich man—how rich he was! And how poor Lazarus! If he had helped him, he would not have missed the money very much, am I not right?" The sin of the wealthy, she argued, is that they choose not to see the needs of the poor. To say that someone is stingy is a profound insult, and a mean person is described as having a narrow heart and thick blood.

Giving and the Honor of the Recipient

However, the interviewees were concerned not only *that* the poor be helped, but that they be helped in a manner which does not compromise the honor of the recipient. Honor is vitally important in Arab society, and if you give a donation but take away the person's honor, you have robbed that person by taking what is more precious than the gift you have given. It is true mercy to protect a person's honor when he is in danger of losing it, especially losing it due to poverty. Abu Nader did not want his son to ask people for money, for that would be shameful. But he believed that if you were to catch a poor person stealing, you would have an obligation to offer him a job or try to find him one. Likewise, Ahmad believed that "we need to help him so that he doesn't steal." Some of the people I interviewed knew Victor Hugo's *Les Miserables*, and they admired the bishop in the candlestick scene, not so much because he saved Jean Valjean from prison, but because he saved him from shame.

> ...if you give a donation but take away the person's honor, you have robbed that person by taking what is more precious than the gift you have given.

As a model of the righteous rich, Marwan chose a television personality who made a documentary on disabled people, teaching the Lebanese to show respect to the disabled. Lara related to me stories of children who, in addition to having to work because of their families' poverty, also had to endure shaming by people better off than themselves who told them they should be in school or that it was a disgraceful thing for a child to have to work. She gave an example of unintentional shaming in which a doctor at a clinic for the poor exclaimed to the mother upon examining a badly infected child, "Why didn't you bring her in before now?!" The unspoken answer was probably that she was afraid she would be told to buy medicine she couldn't afford, or that she, being uneducated, hadn't known what to do, or that she was afraid of being blamed for her daughter's illness. Lara also recounted the story of a desperately poor refugee who went clear across town by bus to get a box of dates because she had heard an organization was distributing them. When she arrived she was asked for her number. It seems the organization was only giving dates in a pre-arranged way to people who had been given numbers. Because she had no number, she was sent home empty-handed, exhausted, and humiliated. This non-government organization (NGO) had meant to bless the poor, but their rigid system had, in this case, dehumanized.

Elias claimed that it is shameful and contrary to piety to beg, even if one has to go without. To ask for help, even from a friend, is humiliating.[453] Maryam claimed, "In my whole life, I have never taken from anyone." Eva especially appreciated the benefactor who frequently left groceries on the table when the family was out and never mentioned it. Elias admired the wealthy person who senses the need of the poor, and helps him "indirectly, in a clever way." The example he offered was paying for the medical insurance of a vulnerable person. He, along with Ahmad, were against giving to professional beggars, who have no sense of shame, and they preferred that people go to foundations for help rather than panhandling on the streets.[454] Zeina said, "There are poor who don't say so, but they are needy; people who can't do for themselves, and people help them without being asked." It is not merely help which the poor need, but help without the impeachment of honor.

Honor, on the other hand, may keep a person from taking work, according to Nayla. To my question, "What is the greatest temptation to the Lebanese people related to money?" she answered, "Work. They won't work at whatever. They are proud. A Lebanese may, if he is overseas, work at whatever, but here in his own country he won't." This was a matter of personal concern for Nayla who earned her living doing the sort of cleaning job normally reserved for despised laborers imported from the third world.

---

[453] This is typical of shame-based societies, according to Sherwood Lingenfelter, *Transforming Culture: A Challenge for Christian Mission* (Grand Rapids: Baker, 1998), 93.

[454] I have heard this often from Syrians and Lebanese. However, people who work for charitable associations assure me that there is not enough money in the coffers to meet the needs of those who are currently asking for help and many truly needy are being turned away or insufficiently helped.

The Gift of Education in Lebanon

The Lebanese have very high literacy rates, and education is extremely important to them. Lebanon's greatest money-producing export is its own children, whose education enables them to find employment overseas and send money back to their families. Adequate education is a strongly felt need in Lebanon. Seventy percent of Lebanese school children attend private schools, as the government schools have a poor reputation. One of the most honorable ways of giving and receiving charity is through education: the building and running of schools, educational scholarships, supply of books and uniforms, and the like. When I began my research in 2005, much was being made of the Hariri Foundation's support of students. Sponsoring a student or convincing the school principal to reduce the student's fees is considered a kindness with lifelong benefit for the recipient's life and family.

Class and Generosity

Some of the lower-class interviewees and those who work with the poor talked about how important it is for the poor to give as well as the rich, even if the gift is something simple indeed. Nayla said, "Wealth is being always able to give, to be able to offer something." She came to the interview with a homemade gift for me. Abu Nader insisted, "If I'm going to have any worth before my children, even if it's something simple, I will help." He took an unpaid holiday to give me the interview, and his family invited me to lunch.

To Zeina the upper-middle class is the preferred position in society in terms of giving, because it entails having sufficient funds to give freely, but greater mobility than the rich person enjoys. While acknowledging that the rich person is in a better position to help because of his wealth and power, Abu Nader actually had more hope that the poor will give. He said, "Maybe the poor person's poverty makes him accept helping those who are suffering. The rich person isn't suffering."[455] Elias described the effects of financial setbacks on his character: "Before, I wasn't like I am now—humble, and I feel with the poor and the unemployed . . ." But the majority of people I asked said that the level of wealth has nothing to do with generosity.

Motives for Giving

One's motive for giving mattered to the Middle Easterners I interviewed. Most advocated giving free of self-interest. Ahmad defined true godliness: "A person gives from his heart, from within, not counting the cost and not thinking, 'Will this get me rich?'" Several of the interviewees, both Muslim and Christian, quoted the saying of Jesus, "Do not let your right hand know what your left hand is doing." It is not unusual for people to give as a compensation for failing in some religious duty such as prayer, financial integrity, or (in the case of Christians) church attendance. This was frowned upon more by the Christians[456] I interviewed than the Muslims. Islam allows for atonement of guilt through giving to the poor, but Muslims warn that such benefactions are not meritorious if they are done with the intent of allowing the donor to continue in his crooked ways with impunity.

Some allowance was made for self-interest in giving. One advantage of giving, according to Eva is that, "if you give to your neighbor, he will give to you." Rana echoed that thought, then told me:

> Giving is very important. If you only do good to the poor, our Lord will look after one of your children in response to your doing this. If you give to the sick person who is unable to pay for treatment and he is healed, God will remove you from your undesirable circumstance. He will take it away from you, if you just give to the poor.

---

[455] Studies done in the UK and US suggest that the poor give more proportionally to charitable organizations than do the rich.
http://www.manchester.ac.uk/discover/news/poor-more-generous-than-rich-in-recession-study-shows
http://www.deseretnews.com/article/865625341/Do-the-poor-give-more-than-the-rich.html
https://www.psychologytoday.com/blog/hidden-motives/201008/why-are-the-poor-more-generous
[456] However, Sudanese and Syrians noted that, while frowned upon in theory, the common practice is for the churches to latch onto such people and exploit their guilt to improve church finances.

During the war in Yemen, Maryam's mother would go without to feed the neighbors *iftar*, the meal to break the fast during Ramadan. Recounting this, Maryam explained, "It is very important that the neighbors see." In Amjad's experience, Muslims and Christians of other denominations have been impressed that his congregation have given to them when their own churches or mosques have failed to do so.

Giving and the Wider Causes of Poverty
Abu Nader was utterly unambiguous and comprehensive in his demands: "We want only one thing from the rich. There shouldn't be poor people on earth." He did not see government responsibility as negating individual responsibility to care for the poor. Using the illustration of a malnourished baby girl, he said, "I am responsible for her. The society is responsible for her." He believed that the pious should band together to contend against the corruption which causes poverty: organized goodness versus organized crime. The wealthy and godly person will not, according to Abu Nader, spend large sums frivolously, but invest them in projects to eliminate poverty or provide assistance to the needy, such as fighting drugs, building schools and clinics, solving Somalia's water shortage problem, or ending the trade in human body parts. Most of the other interviewees spoke of concern for the poor primarily in terms of individual acts of charity. A Sudanese, after holding forth on the arrogance of the rich, admitted there were exceptions "who act, in spite of the fact that they are rich, and who offer to help."

> **Voluntary Poverty for the Sake of the Poor**
> I had in mind the story of Jesus and the rich young ruler, as well as several famous historical accounts of voluntary poverty, when I raised the issue with each interviewee. I framed my question this way: "Imagine that a wealthy person sells his big house and lives in a simple house. He sells his big car and takes public transportation. He gives his money to the poor. Why might he do such a thing? Would such a thing happen in your country?"

Three of the Christian interviewees responding by telling stories of people who had left all to become hermits or monks. Only one of these stories was contemporary. The sole Druze in my sample remembered hearing of a *Khalif* in Egypt who believed everyone should be equal and gave away all the family jewelry to feed the poor. The rest overwhelmingly said no, such a thing was highly unlikely ever to happen. Charlie declared flatly, "It's not in the DNA, unfortunately." In fact, the initial response of all of the Muslims and most of the Christians to the question was a look of total non-comprehension, and in this case, the cause was not my weak Arabic. I expect the rich young ruler adopted a similar facial expression. Nearly all double-checked to be certain they had understood the question, and they had. They made a valiant effort to imagine such voluntary condescension and to speculate on possible motives. Here is what they came up with:

- Sayyid speculated that the money had come from an illicit source, but now the person wants to return to God. In order to start from scratch, he washes his guilt away by selling everything.
- Ahmad reckoned that the person in question had not done anything noteworthy—his original house must have been too big for him, and now he's living at a level appropriate for him.
- Nayla said that he might actually have two houses, but even in that situation, giving one away is unrealistic. Her explanation for his behavior? He must be a fool.
- Zeina suggested two possible reasons for the odd behavior: First, an ascetic, leaving the world to live in simplicity, and second, because his money was causing more problems than it was worth to him. Living simply was his way of getting rid of a headache, a source of trouble.
- Elias put it this way: " . . . the person, having lived the rich life . . . , saw the life of the simple poor, and preferred the simple life which is true Christianity. When one lives

> among nice people, and lots of them, he senses peace of mind and joy. This is the motive."
> - Abu Nader speculated that the person must have done much evil in his lifetime, and knows that death is imminent. He no longer wants anything from this life, and so tries to set right the wrong he has done by giving up his car or villa.
>
> Based on these responses, it seems fair to say that, while generosity with excess income is normative, one cannot assume a Middle Eastern person would understand voluntary poverty for the sake of others. Anyone in the Middle East who tried to sell all and give to the poor should expect to be thought by some a fool or to have some motive of self-interest. At least three of the interviewees mention giving *if one has extra or can afford to give*. I once heard a Muslim instructor teach her circle that it is wrong to give more than one's excess, since giving beyond that would make the giver dependent on the community. Voluntary poverty, then, might not only be perceived as unrealistic by some, but also as irresponsible and therefore, lacking in piety.[457]

In summary, for most Middle Easterners, the righteous rich are rich toward God, either directly, through donations to religious institutions, or indirectly, by giving to the poor as an act of devotion to God. Generous with family and friends, they also do what they can for the truly needy, giving unstintingly to the poor from their surplus wealth. They donate either through charitable foundations or privately, but always in ways that preserve the honor of the recipient. The donations of the righteous rich are nobly motivated and free of political self-interest or show. The righteous of every class are hospitable and generous with their time and interest. They lavish others with welcome, food, and gifts.

---

[457] The exceptions to this generalization were a small but growing number of Arabs who admire certain Western benefactors for sacrificing their wealth in causes like medical research and disaster relief. More on this in chapter 9. Maryam was another exception. She was surprised when she lived in Egypt: "The Egyptians give, but always from what is left. In Yemen, it's the opposite. We always give, and then use the rest."

Generosity and the Bible
Once again, the Bible and Middle Eastern cultural values have much in common. The Bible has a great deal to say about care for the poor and needy. The Prophets leave no doubt that practical, lively concern for the poor is essential to genuine piety. The Word of God opposes giving for self-interest, and the same is true in Middle Eastern popular thought, if not necessarily in practice. Like the Pastoral Epistles, Middle Eastern society insists that those who can should work and not be a burden on society, but that the truly destitute should be taken care of. The Scriptures praise those who are responsible for and openhanded toward family, friends and guests, and despise those who are not.

Hospitality is one of the central themes of Scripture, found repeatedly in direct teaching on the subject, in the overwhelming number of biblical accounts that revolve around situations of hospitality, and in the many parables and metaphors which portray salvation and the kingdom of God in terms of hospitality. Anyone who has lived in the Middle East is able to read the Scripture with deeper insight because the culture of the Middle East saturates its pages.

However, there are at least two points of difference between the Middle Eastern version of caring for the poor and the biblical version. Only a few among the interviewees expressed the sort of passion for systemic justice which characterizes the prophets. Although many complained, people seem unable or unwilling to hold their leaders accountable for justice in the courts, in the expenditure of public funds, and in representation of the interests of the poor. This, in spite of the fact that there are strong grounds for a prophetic stance on the matter in both Islam and Christianity.

Another important difference regards voluntary poverty for the sake of others. Most Arabs can make little sense of the idea. The Scriptures clearly do not demand this of every believer, but neither do they relieve the believer from the duty to hear God's call for sacrifice, even if it means the sacrifice of everything.

Giving in Practice

Since delight in being generous is the hallmark of goodness, we can benefit by self-examination regarding the size of our hearts and the openness of our hands, by repentance and renewal of life in the image of God the ultra-generous. Some questions for self-reflection:
- Do I love to give? Do I go through the day eagerly seeking opportunities to enrich the lives of others?
- Does the awareness of God's generosity to me dominate my thinking about giving and hospitality?
- What are the factors that make me reluctant to give, and what does the Bible say about these things?
- What motivates my giving?
- Is my giving truly a giving of myself?

Westerners tend to be more work-oriented and less socially oriented than Arabs, but relationships are vitally important. Someone who is stingy with time will be diminished in the trust, acceptance, and fruitfulness they enjoy. Anyone who comes to the Middle East should make time to be available to people, to visit and receive visitors. As a task-oriented introvert, I find I need to schedule time for visits and social events as a vital part of my life and work.

Learn the rules of hospitality. In general, the expectations on a host or hostess in the Arab world are more detailed, demanding, and formal than in the West. This may feel burdensome at times, especially if one forgets that the goal of hospitality in the region is to lavish honor on the guest and thereby show oneself to be honorable.

Allow others to give to you. Whether or not they know the teaching of Jesus that "it is more blessed to give than to receive,"[458] most Arabs take the idea seriously, at least when it comes to hospitality. By refusing hospitality or by refusing to let an Arab friend pay from time to time, foreigners deny their friend an opportunity to act honorably. New arrivals in particular should humbly receive and not feel badly about it. There

> **Do I love to give? Do I go through the day eagerly seeking opportunities to enrich the lives of others?**

---
[458] Acts 20:35.

will be chances to reciprocate in time. It is worth remembering that receiving hospitality was one of Jesus' instructions for ministry to his disciples,[459] and his own *modus operandi*. Care for your family and friends. Your credibility depends on how well you do this.

On both biblical and cultural grounds, workers should make a habit of giving generously to the poor. The capacity to give should be taken into account when a worker's funding needs are calculated. Think through and discuss principles and policies of giving with co-workers. As the Bible teaches, donations should be made confidentially, lest the gift humiliate the recipient or serve the ego of the giver. Creative alternatives to cash gifts should be considered, including finding work for a person, arranging educational or medical opportunities, and advocating the needs of the poor among the wealthy. "Do-it-yourself" is not a Middle-Eastern concept: middle- and upper-class people provide jobs for workmen. An unemployed painter will consider you a poor friend if you paint your own living room. When one is unable to give financially, one should still not avoid the needy, but show support in whatever way possible, however symbolic. One example is prayer and fasting for the person.

In my experience, the wealthier are expected to give more than others without being asked. Wade agrees: "You can be a pious person if you're rich or poor, but if you're rich, you should be very, very generous." His informal survey of new believers in Yemen uncovered the fact that many saw the foreigners among them as stingy. The more money the family has, the more food they will bring to social gatherings, often many times what they can possibly eat. Someone who is clearly well off ought to pay the taxi driver an enlarged tip. Sometimes taxi drivers will offer a free ride to a pedestrian who is clearly in tough circumstances. Westerners, who are generally assumed to be well off, should always err on the generous side in giving. I even know one European living in the Arab world who makes a habit of haggling fiercely in the market in order to earn respect that he is not a gullible foreigner, and then pays something near the original asking price because he is able to do so.

---

[459] Luke 10:5–8.

Workers can give and channel outside funds through charitable foundations run by themselves, local churches, or NGOs. A great deal of self-discipline is needed in operating these foundations as Middle Easterners in general expect little in the way of accountability. This can be a great source of frustration for Westerners with Middle Eastern bosses, co-workers, employees, or voluntary workers. Schools and clinics in poor areas fulfill a need that is felt especially strongly, but be prepared for the motives behind the institution to be tested, and sometimes maligned.

Workers who take a big drop in income in order to serve should not expect understanding, gratitude, or applause from Middle Easterners. On the contrary, they should be prepared for suspicion about their motives or even their sanity. Any worker who chooses to live notably below the level at which he or she is able to live should expect to be misunderstood by both ordinary Middle Eastern people and the authorities.[460] This is not to say one should not do so, but one should know that the cost involved is greater than merely the cost of physical deprivation.

The Western worker in the Middle East will quickly learn that matters of corruption, legal justice, financial management, and human rights are handled differently in the Middle East than in the homeland. As a guest in the country, the foreign worker would do well to make sure that he or she has understood the political and social situation thoroughly from a variety of Middle Eastern perspectives before making public comments or criticism. However, it is often appropriate to ask questions in the role of the innocent observer: How does it work? Who benefits by it? How does it affect the poor? Do you think God approves or disapproves? What are you going to do about it?

Although interviewees spoke about Syrian and Iraqi refugees due to the current crisis, some of the poorest people in the region were hardly mentioned: migrant domestic workers and manual laborers from impoverished parts of Asia and Africa, Gypsies, and (in Lebanon and Syria) Palestinian refugees. These are often treated as unworthy to receive either generosity or honor. Workers can

---

[460] Mallouhi, *Miniskirts*, 29–30.

teach in word and deed their Middle Eastern friends and associates to demonstrate true piety in their relationship with these despised groups. There are also Middle Easterners who work for justice in the courts and through appeals to government officials for more just laws on behalf of the marginalized. Workers might encourage them by taking their advice, offering services where appropriate, praying for them, standing with them, supporting their causes financially, or connecting them with international human rights organizations.

Concern for the poor is a fruitful topic for bridging conversations between followers of Jesus and other Middle Easterners. Many Muslims in those Middle Eastern countries with a significant Christian minority can quote one or two of Jesus' better known teachings about money. There are many points of agreement, and much to affirm, but also differences which bear consideration. In particular, Muslims will be both impressed and repulsed by the absurdly high demands of Jesus regarding money, and his incarnational grace, "that though he was rich, yet for your sakes, he became poor, so that through his poverty might become rich."[461]

The refugee crisis resulting from the conflicts in Iraq, Sudan, and Syria has stretched both the giving and the vision of churches throughout the region. Until recently Middle Eastern churches generally restricted their giving to the needy of their own denominations, though there were some notable exceptions. It has become normal for many churches now to devote themselves to giving to the practical care of people who would have been shunned only a decade or so ago. Although it can occasionally be politically sensitive, in most cases aid organizations and churches value the participation, support, and fund-raising efforts of trusted foreigners. Workers with a world consciousness can help the churches become aware of needs farther afield, and encourage greater participation in the needs and ministries of the world-wide church. Church planters and those workers who have a teaching role in the body of Christ should ensure that their teaching does justice to the biblical demands to care for the poor and to protect their rights.[462]

---

[461] 2 Corinthians 8:9.
[462] Ronald J. Sider, *Rich Christians in an Age of Hunger: A Biblical Study* (Downers Grove: Intervarsity, 1980), 208–209.

6

Money: Where Did It Come From?

The source of one's wealth matters. All of my interviewees asked the question which forms the title of this chapter. They felt uneasy giving endorsement to a person as "the pious rich" unless they knew how the person had become rich. From Iraqis to Sudanese, Middle Easterners recite the query, "From where did this come to you?" (*min ayna laka hadha?*). Glades explained that the phrase is part of traditional and contemporary culture ("You even see it on the serials!") and law ("the government can ask anyone this question about his possessions"). In some areas, such as the Levant region, people don't hesitate to ask directly about the source of a person's income, whereas in other areas, such as Yemen, people simply wonder and scrutinize one's life for clues to the answer.

Interviewees were particularly eager to apply this question with regard to politicians[463] and men of religion.[464] Abu Nader accused all politicians of being crooks and wondered about their mysterious acquisitions of wealth. He asked, "Is this piety? Or is this [dramatic pause] ah-ha! profit!"

---

[463] Foreign residents of Lebanon are required to sign a statement promising not to criticize any government except the government of Israel. I wish to point out that criticisms of any government made in this book do not originate with me. I am merely reporting what I have been told by citizens of the countries of the region. I have not voiced my own views.

[464] The term "men of religion" (*rajil dīn*) is widely used in the region as an inclusive term for clergy and religious workers of every type, including nuns. As a female seminary professor and pastor, I have a residency visa in Lebanon as a "man of religion." Female clergy are rare in the region, limited, to my knowledge, to Druze female *'aqqāl* and a handful of Protestant pastors.

Men of Religion

Nearly everyone had an opinion about the clergy: their lifestyles, their integrity, and the level of corruption among them. Men of religion received mixed reviews. On the positive side:

- Lara, a Christian, said that, although it was rare for sheikhs to visit the desperately poor and nominally Muslim shantytown which her NGO runs in Lebanon, members of the community turn to the sheikhs confidently when there is an emergency.
- Most of the Sudanese I talked to said most of their men of religion are honest and respected, and if they have a bit more than those around them, it is only because of the gifts of appreciation they receive from their congregations.
- Atallah, also a Christian, spoke highly of the sheikhs in southern Syria as being trustworthy men of integrity and respect. His compatriot Maya added that they do not take advantage of the people.

Some were ambiguous:

- Rabia from Egypt noted that often the clergy were somewhat better off than the people because they often came from moneyed families and had the advantage of inherited wealth.
- Egyptians differed from one another about the extent to which clergy exploit the advantages of their profession, and particularly the respect, privileges, and discounts offered to them daily because of their status.
- Fouad said that a few Sudanese Christian clergy have wealth or have undertaken projects which seem beyond their means. But people only bring up these apparent discrepancies when they are in conflict with a leader. Accusations of dishonesty among the clergy are usually a sign more of a breakdown of relationship than of genuine concern about dishonesty.

There were a number of negative reactions as well:

- Most of the Lebanese I talked to had reservations about some clergy[465] whose lifestyles, they believe, are significantly more luxurious than the lifestyles of those they serve. Abu Nader said, "There might be some very small percentage which are poor in the beginning, but they all have money. I haven't seen a man of religion, be he Muslim, Christian, or Druze, but he has money. How can one say that they are really pious when one doesn't know whence their affluence springs?"
- Representatives of all sects in Lebanon suspected some religious leaders of dipping into funds intended for charitable work.
- From Sudan: "Our Evangelical churches, if there is a pastor who has money, the people have doubts about his affairs. They say maybe he is stealing from the church. Maybe he has a project that is built upon the back of the church."
- Eva had little good to say about men of religion. She told me, "They use their power to prey on the people."
- Elias believed that the priesthood has become such a lucrative profession that many priests enter the ministry "to secure their futures," rather than from any true sense of calling.
- From upper Egypt: "There are people, priests or sheikhs—from both sides—as soon as they take this image, they force something on you against your will, in order to be central in the town or village. Not all of them are pious. People become their victims."
- "Have you ever seen a man of religion who was not driving a late-model car? Have you ever seen a man of religion with a press-button phone? They all have three or four cellular phones." "If someone is divorcing his wife, he's going to take $20,000, $30,000, $100,000 from him in the court ... They're stealing who take that much." (Lebanese youth)

---

[465] But not all. Abu Nader, with characteristic sweeping language, vilified the entire religious establishment as extravagant, but all the others allow, with varying degrees of conviction, for humble and honest men of religion.

Zeina brings the question, "Where did it come from?" home. She wants to ensure that any material gain within the family has been acquired by proper means. As a Sunni Muslim, she weighed the source of any income by whether it is permitted (*halal*) or forbidden (*haram*). The explanation she gave in her interview is worth quoting at length.

Karen: Do you see a relationship between wealth and piety?
Zeina: [Softly, as though to herself] Treasure. The one who fears God. [Aloud] Yes. And he doesn't take forbidden money. He doesn't steal, for instance. And if he has permitted (halal) money, he is very sensitive about it.
Karen: What is permitted money?
Zeina: That is money that you take from your work. For what is proper. Stealing: it's money that is forbidden (haram). If one stole money, or if one worked for a company and he took something from the company, that is forbidden. For instance, if he took something to sell it for himself. This is forbidden. Is there not a God who sees you? You are taking something which is not yours that you should benefit from it. If there is something that is yours and you benefit from it, that is permitted. Now, the money that you put in the bank, a percentage comes to you.
Karen: Interest?
Zeina: Interest. Some say it is forbidden and some say that it is permitted. I take it and give it to poor people. The money that comes from the bank, I don't want it. I just want *my* money. I don't like to keep money in the house where I might lose it or something, so I put it in the bank and it stays with them. But, when it comes to the interest money, I don't know how the bank has worked with it. Some of them put it into a company for trade. But does that company break its promises a lot? If they make a clean profit, that money is acceptable, but some get hold of money and get out, and that money was the money of orphans. That is forbidden. I don't want to put my money with people I don't know. Even if I do know them, there are people who see money and multiply it and steal from the people with it. That's what makes

one afraid. I like the money to be halal. I want to know what has been done with it, and then I can spend it.

Karen: I interrupted you when you were explaining what the relationship is between godliness and wealth.

Zeina: Godliness is when you fear God. You fear that the money which you take is proper.

Karen: Halal?

Zeina: Halal. Money that is halal. This is your fear.

Zeina explained her fear about forbidden and permitted money later in the interview, quoting a proverb, "Forbidden money goes, and so does its owner." She interpreted the proverb this way: "It means if you get money, sometimes it burns. For example, if you built a house with money that wasn't halal, it might burn down. Or something like that. Whereas the halal money lasts."

> Forbidden money goes, and so does its owner.

All of the Muslim interviewees shared Zeina's concern about haram and halal. Most were unable to give the sort of specifics given by Zeina, an imam's daughter, but they were clear that money gained through hard work or inheritance is permitted. Between them, they produced an extensive list of illicit means through which haram money is gained: theft, exploitation, forming mafias, prostitution, selling stolen or faulty goods, failing to return excess change given by mistake, gambling and the lottery,[466] laundering money, receiving bribes, taking money under the table to avoid taxes, taking more than is due, treachery, killing for hire, counterfeiting money, selling drugs, and deception. Among Palestinians, money gained from the sale of land to Israel is haram.

According to Rana, "Whatever you do with haram money, even if you spend it for halal, it stays haram. All money that you get by halal, if you spent it for haram, it becomes haram." There was an uncertain agreement among interviewees that a poor person who takes donations is not held accountable by God for how the donor

---

[466] Rana explained why the lottery is haram: "Because the money comes suddenly, and this way, I'm taking it from a lot of people. The prize that I won doesn't belong to me, so that is haram."

acquired the money, and that the poor make it a practice not to ask. Men of religion, according to Ahmad, have a duty to study the Qur'an and Hadith or the Gospel carefully because they must be experts on haram and halal.[467] Muhammad summed it up, "There is nothing sweeter than halal in everything!"

Christians shared many of the same concerns. Ammar from Sudan was taught, "if you eat from a stolen spoon in your trade, you'll be finished—even the spoon will go!" His friend Daoud told of a Christian owner of a supermarket, a man of integrity, whose supermarket succeeded because he had people's trust while all around other supermarkets went under.

Several Christians quoted with bitterness the saying, "The money of the Nasrani [Christians] is halal,"[468] by which Christians understand that Muslims can steal from Christians with impunity according to Islamic law. The Muslims I have asked have denied this vehemently, but many Christians are convinced it is so. Fouad was grateful that the vast majority of Muslims were raised with a piety, in his view, superior to that of their official religion. Ram, a believer in Jesus from a Muslim family, was of two minds about the source of money in Islamic society:

> [Islam teaches] Don't love this world but love the next. Do for the other. Treat the world as though you were going to live a long time, and treat the end as though you were going to die tomorrow. But at the same time, the stories in Islam, how they made money, very much encourage the opposite—in negative ways. The incursions ("openings") and the spoils that they were taking by force. To finance the war, they were taking from the enemy. It was clear that material things were something important for them. During one invasion they lost because they forgot the war and went to take the spoils. There is love of money, but at the same time there is much in the Qur'an that says don't love money very much.

---

[467] Christians frequently use these distinctively Muslim terms in a non-technical sense. Nayla asked rhetorically about the well-known Rafiq al-Hariri, "But the foundation of his fortune–I ask you–is it 100% correct, 100% legitimate, 100% halal?" The Sunday prior to my writing this paragraph, I heard a Protestant preacher criticize immature Christians "who cannot distinguish between halal and haram." The one Druze interviewee also used these terms.

[468] Christians in the region also quote, also against Muslim objections, the twin and chilling saying, "The blood of the Christians is halal."

Amjad also found Muslims inconsistent: "The government has a side which leans toward religious talk, but there's a sort of schizophrenia. There is talk of religion, but also financial corruption." Amjad admitted it wasn't only the Muslims: "We all say the same words. Someone will be participating in financial corruption and he'll say, 'The livelihood is from God.'"

The most common proverb I heard from Shi'ites in the course of my research is the saying of Imam Ali: "One only amasses a fortune through stinginess or theft." Abu Nader, therefore, held in suspicion anyone very rich. Even if the money was inherited, how did the father or the grandfather come by it? Nayla shared his suspicions. She said of one politician's wealth, "God knows. But I think that even if a person worked however long every month, the Lord will not give him this fortune." A Syrian told about a situation in which the recipient of a generous gift had his reputation besmirched because of his sudden rise in wealth. The donor had wished to keep the gift quiet, but, as a result, rumors spread that the recipient was a thief. Many Middle Easterners seem to follow the rule, "When in doubt, assume the worst."

> **One only amasses a fortune through stinginess or theft.**

No one had any doubt, however, about the importance of work as a legitimate way of acquiring wealth. For Eva, not only is work halal, it is evidence of character, self-respect, and love for one's family. Interviewees agreed that most people want to work and are reluctant to be dependent on others, but there are always exceptions, and these exceptions are not viewed well. Sadly, not all honest work is considered respectable in much of the Middle East, even if it is halal, and a poor person may have to make the terrible choice between total destitution for his family or taking a job which will humiliate them, such as cleaning toilets or shining shoes.

Pessimism about the Current Economic Climate

Work, even honorable work, isn't likely to get a person far. Most of the interviewees agreed that a small minority are able to improve their economic lot through legitimate work, but they are the exceptions. A few skillful traders, specialist doctors, and singers do well. Otherwise, inheritance is about the only permissible source of wealth in our times. Nearly everyone I interviewed considered himself or herself middle class, from the professional with a villa and a live-in maid to the penniless student. Yet nearly all also agreed that the middle class is disappearing and leaving a huge gap between the extremely wealthy, one might say the filthy rich, and the oppressed, vast majority. The comments below represent the economic outlook of ordinary Middle Easterners:

- There was a day when people would be able to buy lands and the world was beautiful. Now, because of the economic situation, it is hard for a person to own land, unless he has inherited land from his forebears. (Sudan)
- It used to be that most of the people rented, but now many own their homes and have become middle class. (a different region of Sudan)
- Either someone has to have connections, or steal, or be the director of a bank, and even the director of a bank doesn't have money any longer. Now the person who wants to live well has to travel. It is no longer the case that he can live in Lebanon and have money. [I replied, "This is something that makes the heart mourn." The response: This is Lebanon].
- Louisa, also Lebanese, had family members working in the Arabian Peninsula because suitable jobs are rare in Lebanon. She sadly compared the struggles of the Lebanese with the life she had in Saudi Arabia or the UAE, and particularly noted the personal and economic debt of the Lebanese. Her assessment: "I don't see any improvement plan for the country by *any* minister. We

> are the same since 1987: Electricity, fuel, water, sewage system, vehicles, roads, the infrastructure—everything."
> - Charlie, another Lebanese: "I would tell you something that may surprise you. The days of the civil war were better economically than today. The economy was robust. People had more money. Okay, people were getting killed because they were shooting one another, but I'm talking economically. And the country survived 15 years of the civil war, but now . . . !"
> - "People divide up their incomes into money for the household and money for *qat* [a mild stimulant]. Sometimes they have nothing to eat, because it has all gone to buy *qat*." (Yemen)
> - "Things are definitely getting worse. The economic situation of Christians is better than that of Muslims in Palestine, as they receive more for their work."
> - The situation is on the floor. If the mentality of the people doesn't change, nothing is going to happen. (Lebanese youth)
> - In these last so many years we've had ISIS, the draining of the government funds, and the proliferation of corruption in the Iraqi government. (Iraq)
> - There aren't many who are very wealthy. The majority of the rich left, because for them it was possible. (Iraq)
> - Sin and money? Who has money that they can use it badly?! (Egypt)

In a survey I conducted in Lebanon in 2005, twenty-six out of the 109 examples given of the evil rich focused on the means of getting wealth or its inappropriate accumulation. Most popular was the accusation against government personalities of theft and misappropriating public funds. Others included gaining wealth through bribery and corruption, murder, lying, and using people. One wrote scornfully of a well-known leader, "He doesn't know how to work." By contrast, three respondents specifically praised rich people they knew (or knew of) for gaining their wealth through hard work. The second-most quoted proverb (nine from 103 responses), and the most popular Muslim quotation, was the one mentioned above, given by Abu Nader, "Wealth is not amassed except by haram or stinginess."[469] Ram from Palestine agreed: "A person who walks in piety and doesn't already have a lot of money, it is hard for him to come into money."

> **Bribery and Corruption**
> According to Transparency International's 2016 Perception of Corruption Index, only two nations in the Middle East and North Africa (Qatar and UAE) managed more than a 50% score for integrity. They reported that half of the world's ten most corrupt nations are found in the region: Iraq, Libya, Sudan, Yemen, and Syria. There is every indication that corruption is increasing dramatically.[470]
>
> Most interviewees were eager to tell me about it. Some made general complaints:
>
> - When I used the word "bribery," with a group of Syrians, one exclaimed, "That's a study all by itself!" and the others all laughed and nodded.
> - Another Syrian said, "We are a bribed nation," to which yet another added, "Beginning with the church and the mosque." Still another said, "Anything you want to do, there is bribery in it."
> - In Syria, bribery isn't mentioned directly, but is called, "a gift," or "a cup of coffee." Egyptians call it "a glass of tea," "jasmine," or "oil." In many countries of the region, it is called a "tip" (*bakhshīsh* or *ikrāmiyah*).
> - People from a number of countries apportion partial blame for the rampant corruption to the low salaries for government employees. Since officials cannot live on

---

[469] Compare this to John Chrysostom's declaration that "the root and origin of private riches was always to be found in some injustice or rapine." Kidd, *Wealth and Beneficence*, 47, quoting from Ossowski, *Class Structure*, 32, who refers to Chrysostom's Homily 12 on 1 Timothy.
[470] https://www.transparency.org/news/feature/mena_a_very_drastic_decline

the salary they receive, they refuse to do their work until compensated by the person they are supposed to be serving.
- A man from South Sudan reckoned up to one third of a person's income must be given over to extortion by various government officials in order to get the papers one needs to live a normal life.[471]
- On bribery: "It has become part of the kingdom, the same as Yemeni-ness. Life isn't going to go ahead without it. It is a normal thing, even normal among the believers." (Yemen)
- The only way to become rich in Lebanon? "To be a thief. A governmental thief. Truly, all of the leaders are thieves . . . and also the government employees and the employees of the hospitals who do accounts. If your cost is 1 million lira, he writes 10 million and keeps 9. Your life doesn't concern him. You have to be a thief in Lebanon to have money." (Lebanese youth)
- [Asking about sins related to money, I mentioned bribery.] Bribery? All of us do it. The poor do it. All economic levels do it. No, bribery doesn't enter into it [that is, into the category "sin."] Bribery is going to be given—it's not in your hand to change that. (The same Lebanese youth)
- At the least, if you want to finish anything in the government, buy him some qat. (Yemen)
- There are many who have relatives who are influential and, although below middle class, they were suddenly elevated because of corruption. (Iraq)

Others told their own stories:

- A taxi driver complained that he would frequently be stopped for inspection. Even if there was nothing wrong with his car, he would be forced to wait the entire day unless he greased the official's palm.

---
[471] In 2016, South Sudan dropped down to the second worst ranking in Transparency's Perception of Corruption Index: 175th out of 176 countries: https://www.transparency.org/news/feature/corruption_perceptions_index_2016

- "When there is a rich person, I mean really rich, there are two questions which always present themselves to our minds: 'From where?' and 'Why him and not me?' I heard it from people who are believers and they were accusing him of theft, but from inside they were saying, 'Why him and not me?' I mean, 'Why did he steal and I didn't steal and I didn't get this house?'"
- Muhammad, a Syrian refugee, claimed $2000 was taken from him by a Lebanese government official, and he was warned that asking for it back could cost him his life.
- A Sudanese shopkeeper told of losing his shop because he was unwilling to pay bribes.
- "The guy who was running our development project and controlling our visa, whenever we traveled, we would come back with a very nice gift for him. That way, when we were signing papers, it was never like there was something 'other.' We would kind of preempt [bribery] with a nice gift. That was a way that we could do it without feeling that we were contributing to the corruption in the system." (Yemen)
- "My mother, when she wanted to finish my papers for me, so that the papers would be finished today, you pay money, and it's finished. Or, it could be finished in two months. So, in order to finish my papers, she did it, but my mother was troubled." (Yemen)
- An Iraqi asked why there were so many aid agencies opening and some were being operated by youths with little apparent financial backing. He knew the government wasn't contributing. Upon inquiring, he discovered that referral agencies "give them, like, $10,000" as start-up money. He laughed. "To every new organization. So that's the secret."
- How do people become rich? "They get a job with the government because they have a relative in the government, and they employ more relatives. They get a commission for every government project they run, and profit by using two different budgets. A government

minister makes an NGO in his wife's name, and all the funds go to that NGO." (Iraq)
- Years ago, a Syrian recounted how he once dealt with corruption in a government office. His papers were completely in order and had been submitted weeks previously, but whenever he went in to ask about the document he was waiting for, he was told by the official it wasn't ready yet. All his friends agreed that the official was holding out for a bribe. One day, after he had been told yet again that his document wasn't ready, he said in a pleasant voice, but loud enough for all the citizens and officials in the crowded office to hear, "I submitted this request months ago. You tell me there is no problem, but still I wait. The only explanation I can think of is that you want a bribe. If that is what you want please say so." His document became ready within the week.

In the minds of most Middle Easterners, then, the righteous rich are an endangered species. Abu Nader reckons it is impossible to be rich and godly. Even an unquestionably generous man like Rafik al-Hariri sullied his reputation for piety by amassing wealth through undisclosed means.

In sum, the righteous rich person works hard for his or her income and does not use a political or religious position to access money for personal lifestyle enhancement. He or she studiously avoids any hint of theft, selling stolen or faulty goods, bribery, gambling, money laundering, prostitution, overcharging, embezzlement, deception, and the like. If one is to be considered righteous by conservative Muslims, he or she will not derive income from interest or from the profit of companies engaged in questionable business practices.

> **In the minds of most Middle Easterners, then, the righteous rich are an endangered species.**

The Source of Wealth and the Bible

God shares with Arabs a serious concern about how people acquire money. The Law and the Proverbs are full of teaching about what is acceptable and what is not. The prophetic tradition gives ample precedent for asking hard questions to the rich about the source of their prosperity. The Word of the Lord finds a strong echo in Nayla's question, "Is there not a God who sees you?" The Scriptures also show the same healthy tension as did the interviews about God being the source of wealth, his punishment in this life of those who gain through evil means, and the fact that often the wicked prosper.

Once again, my concerns with the interviews take the form of omissions. Virtually nothing was said by any of the interviewees about God the Judge and the accounting of the Last Day, although these beliefs are vital both to Islam and to Christianity. For those in the prophetic tradition, like Amos, Jesus, and James, the coming judgment gives their message great authority and urgency. Perhaps if Middle Eastern people returned to this conviction with all their hearts, they would find themselves empowered to contend with the corruption they bemoan among their leaders. This omission also suggests the need for more explicit teaching which connects the doctrine of divine judgment with daily life.

Of course, God's judgment falls upon all people, not only the leaders. I was impressed with Zeina's careful application to her own family life of the standards of integrity she believes in. The other interviewees were very quick to point the finger at the rich and famous, but had little to say about how they manage to live righteously in the context of the ethical dilemmas they face in making money. It is human nature that people talk about rules or principles and apply them critically to others, but are evasive or defensive in assessing themselves. In fact, the corruption which is so obvious in the mighty also pervades the lives of ordinary workers. God addresses his righteous demands to both great and small.

While none of the interviewees fell into this trap in an obvious way, I do see a danger in the halal versus haram dichotomy in that it could promote an emphasis on pleasing God through what is external and measurable. If Ahmad believes that the gospel is primarily a list of do's and don'ts, he has missed the point of the gospel. Lists of rules can be worked around without breaking the letter of the law. A subtle love of money is the root of all kinds of evil.

The Source of Money in Practice
Obviously, God's servant should avoid any sinful means of obtaining money. However, most cultures have habitual sins related to money, such as consumerism in the West, and may vary substantially on what is considered acceptable. When I lived in Syria, virtually no one considered it wrong to slip a few lira to the policeman to avoid being fined for a traffic violation, but dividing up the bill between friends at a restaurant nearly ranked with patricide in the list of unspeakable evils. Okay, I exaggerate—slightly.

Foreign workers may find themselves expected to turn a blind eye to what they believe is wrong, particularly by national religious leaders. One example is the use of designated funds for other purposes: money donated for clothes for the orphans might be used to wine and dine a politician with the justification that without that politician's support the orphanage could be closed. Particularly when the worker is in a subservient position, there are no easy answers. As always, it is important to understand the situation thoroughly and not make rash judgments.

Workers may also find that practices which are normal for them are seen as questionable or even haram by some Middle Easterners, particularly conservative Muslims. In all of these situations, it is right to ask what the Word of God says. What does God think about me "earning" interest from a bank which forecloses on home loans given to the poor? Am I morally responsible for investing in companies whose subsidiaries produce nuclear weapons, exploit the poor, or produce products harmful to the body, the environment, the society, or the spirit? It is not well to assume that the Muslims among whom we live are always our moral inferiors or that we have nothing to learn from them. Even when a worker personally has no moral qualms about a given means of gaining income, it is worth considering how that means is perceived by others. Trade in general may be halal, but the Muslims of Sidon, for example, prevented the opening of a major supermarket in their city until they obtained legal assurances that the store would be closed if it sold any pork products or alcohol. Another example: not many Arabs would label as pious someone who profited from shares in a weapons manufacturer that sold arms to Israel.

Stinginess is seen in the Middle East as an irreverent way of amassing money. Given the different standards Arabs have compared to Westerners regarding generosity and hospitality, it would be a valuable exercise for workers to try to perceive themselves as their neighbors perceive them.

Most expatriate workers dread the inevitable questions people ask about the source and amount of their income. We find these questions intrusive. Sometimes they are a cause of embarrassment, such as when the worker does not want it to be known that he or she is supported by Christian churches in the West. The temptation is to be evasive in answering, and most Middle Easterners will give up asking aloud after receiving a few non-committal answers. However, these interviews suggest that some people will go on asking the questions among themselves, assuming that we have something we wish to hide, something ignoble and not in keeping with piety. The problem is further complicated by the fact that some of those who ask have no frame of reference to understand a frank answer. On more than one occasion I have been grilled about our source of income and have carefully explained about supporting churches and individuals, only to be asked, "So the U.S. government pays you, right?" Once again, there is no simple solution, but it helps to know that Middle Eastern people are suspicious, and to some degree they have a right to be. New workers should be warned before arrival to be prepared with a suitable answer.

Missionaries should not assume that, because they are obviously religious people, they will be respected for their piety regardless of class status. On the contrary, the interviews make clear that wealth among religious people can be highly suspect and a source of resentment. Men of religion have a greater obligation than the average citizen to be transparent about whence they have acquired their wealth. New workers would do well to take very seriously the advice of national pastors and other church leaders in the matter of lifestyle, but also to use a little caution. The lack of respect expressed by ordinary middle- and lower-class Middle Easterners in the interviews for their religious leaders accounts for some of my reservations. One may have to decide in some circumstances if he or she prefers to gain acceptance by the senior clergy or the people. In addition, Christian religious leaders are susceptible to the same sinful cultural patterns by which other religious and political leaders live.

However, Pastor Charlie advises foreign Christians not to be too concerned about others' opinions of them:

> The problem is, people talk. If you are a missionary and you live on little money, people will accuse you of being stingy and stashing the money away for your retirement. If you splurge, they say, "Hah! He's a Western missionary. Of course, he's got millions being funneled to him." So you're damned if you do and damned if you don't. Bottom line: Live as God would have you live in good conscience. Be hospitable, as hospitable as you can. Be generous with others, and don't listen to what people say. When you've done those things, you can ignore what people say.

For tentmakers, it is essential that business practices be above reproach, and that there is not a hint of gaining money through questionable means.[472] Foreign workers in business will find this a great challenge, but it is the same challenge that devout Middle Eastern people face daily. Talking through the ethics of practical situations with local people could be a platform for discussion of other religious issues.

There is a felt need in the churches for practical training in conducting business successfully as a believer, taking into account the realities of the market and the corruption endemic in the system. This is best done by a local merchant with an excellent reputation, but such a person may never have considered the possibility of teaching or mentoring other disciples of Jesus as business people.

---

[472] John White, *The Golden Cow: Materialism in the Twentieth-Century Church* (Downers Grove: Intervarsity, 1979), 61.

Such a person might also need some encouragement and training in thinking theologically about business, so that their own teaching is thoroughly grounded in the Scriptures. At a simpler level, many families, especially among the poor, need training in how to get out of debt, live within their means, respond to extortion, manage money, save, and work toward realistic financial goals.

Workers who gain their livelihood by raising support have an obligation before God to do so with integrity, not exaggerating their efforts and successes, or using manipulative ploys, or exploiting local believers' ministries and conversions to enhance their own income.[473]

In light of the widespread economic needs and ubiquitous corruption, people of vision and courage are needed in ministries of creating employment opportunities, fostering wholesome foreign investments, and speaking prophetically about and working against corruption.

---

[473] I know of several cases in the region in which Westerners have exploited others for financial gain in ways such as implying falsely that they had a role in someone's conversion, video-taping someone else's school and clinic and showing the video in Europe as a presentation of their own work, and asking a congregation to raise their hands if they love Jesus and displaying the video of those raised hands in the US as though each hand represented a conversion.

7

Appearances

"Not everyone who spends money is rich," Rana pointed out. My years of experience living in the Middle East have given me the impression that appearances are both very important and very deceptive. This is why I made it a point to ask two questions regarding appearances. The first was: "Are there people in your country who pretend to be wealthier than they are?" For no other question did I find the responses so clearly distinguished according to country. All of the Lebanese agreed heartily that examples abound. Some visibly warmed to the subject, as though to say, "Now here's a question I'd love to answer!" All of the interviewees from other countries who had lived in Lebanon described the Lebanese in exactly the same way as the Lebanese perceived themselves. It was also unanimous that the Lebanese are premier in the Middle East for this sort of pretension. As we shall see, it does exist in other Arab nations, but in none is it so marked as in the land of the cedar.

My second question related to appearances was the opposite of the first: "Are there people who pretend to be poorer than they are?" Here it was the Egyptians who became animated, and, to a lesser degree, the Sudanese, the Syrians, and those who work with refugees. It seems, though, that there are people who play poor in every country. While many of the interviewees saw that affecting a false economic status upward or downward is common, none suggested that he or she personally engages in such affectation.

The Appearance of Less Wealth
"You have, and yet you give the appearance of not having: this is our nature, and this nature is a problem," an Egyptian told me.

Those who give the appearance of having less than they do are found throughout the region and at every economic level. Middle Eastern society in general does not allow individuals and families much privacy, and it is normal for people to gossip about others' lifestyles and possessions.[474] Many of the interviewees spoke about the constant awareness they feel that people are watching them, and it became clear through their comments that some, at least, are keen observers of others. Marwan told me, "If a person has money, right away it becomes known." Louisa felt it was not always obvious at first, but the discrepancy comes to light with time:

> Some people hide. "We don't have." When you hear them, you believe them. But once you look at the way they are living, you start wondering. The cars they own, the schools that their children are in—all this costs money! Traveling, tourism, and these things, and then they say, "We don't have money." How come? It's very hard logically to accept it.

What would motivate such behavior? Among the Lebanese, middle-class Elias saw these as clever people who are trying to avoid being victims of theft and other crimes which thrive in the current difficult economic climate. The lower-class interviewees begged to differ. Nayla ascribed their behavior to greed and hypocrisy. Abu Nader called them liars and accused them of tightfistedness toward relatives and the needy. He claimed that many well-known people fall into this category. The Egyptians saw the pretense of poverty as very common in their society and described it as the cunning way that people with some means prey on the compassion of the unsuspecting and get charity they would not be given if the donor had known the truth about their financial situation.

The Syrians had a variety of explanations for a downwardly mobile pretense, which they believed to be far more common in their country than its opposite. Eva and Muhammad thought that it was a widespread practice for people with money to deny that they have it.

---

[474] This trait isn't unique to the Middle East by any means. However, the Westerner might be surprised at the degree to which people observe and comment on the lifestyle choices of others.

Why? "So that their relatives don't ask from them. They don't want anyone to ask for help." Maya added three more possible reasons a person might act poorer than he is in reality: 1) so that people won't envy him, 2) because his family is from a lower class than his current income and he is more comfortable with the simple life of his family, and 3) so that he won't be robbed.

When there is a large amount of aid available in a region, this sort of artifice becomes widespread. Ram said about his homeland of Palestine:

> Certainly it [pretending poverty] is present. Why? Because there are many who help the Palestinian people. It is known that the Palestinian people are always asking for money. [Said with an embarrassed smile]. People very much like to appear as though they don't have in order to get the money, to get the aid, to get the clothes. This is a big problem with us, unfortunately. Many poor people lose out on the aid money because of rich people who appear not to have.

A Story from Egypt

I was the pastor. An elderly woman came to me, greeted me, and began to cry: "I haven't got any money." When I went to the house, there was no furniture. I didn't have money in my pocket, so I went up and knocked on the doors [of people from the church], and asked. I said, "So-and-so is down below and she wants money." And the person thought and told me, "Don't give her money." I asked, "Why?" He said, "She has money." I said, "She hasn't got any." He said, "She has." I said, "She hasn't. I have decided." So he said, "That's it. You want to." So he brought out money and loaned it to me to give to her.

I came to her after two days, and discovered she was building another story for the house! Very often the people complain that there isn't any money, but there is exploitation in the matter. I didn't sleep that first night thinking about this

> woman without food. And the evidence is that she has been drawing, drawing, drawing from the people, saving money in order to build. After six months she came and argued with me, saying, "I built a story: Why are you not helping me to finish it?" I said, "I have been renting an apartment outside [*the country*] for 500 guineas for 15 years." Five hundred guineas is a large sum, and she is building her own home and she wants money!

The Appearance of Greater Wealth

> Whenever I return I see people. You sense them. . . . When you enter their home, their home is empty, there isn't anything; their house is disorderly. They haven't got money. They have a debt over them. Their car, for instance, is the bank's. Their salary isn't very high, but you look from outside and you think, "Wow! How he dresses! What he writes! What he does!" (Palestine)

Lebanon represents the extreme in the region of concern for appearances. Lara said, for example, "I was shocked, when I came to Lebanon, at the level of classism. It still unnerves me. In Jordan your honor often comes from what tribe you're from versus your class." Although the focus of much of the material that follows is on Lebanon, people also feign greater wealth than they possess elsewhere in the Middle East. Among the upper class of Palestine, Iraq, Yemen, and Egypt, it is important to maintain an image.

Although uncommon in upper Egypt, according to Emad, the urban life of Cairo has fostered envy and a competitive spirit which drives people to compare themselves with others and to seek to get on the higher level. "In Egypt," Nivin said, "money creates an intrapersonal cacophony. It makes the other person say, 'O Professor, O Professor.' Money gives worth, it gives one a place." Nevertheless, according to Karam, many Egyptians view the rich as those who have robbed the country, as the corruptors, and as the cause of the national economic problems. At least in the presence of the majority of Egyptians who are not well-off, "the rich person doesn't look at his wealth as something to be proud of," he told me.

> **Tribe Rather than Class in Jordan**
> Lara told this story. "In Jordan you can be from a certain tribe, but very poor: it doesn't matter. I remember one time on the highway we were driving, and we missed an exit, so the driver reversed, and almost hit a man. The guy was a bit shocked, standing on the roadside, and he knocked on the window. He was very angry. He said, 'You know, I'm not a cat. I'm from Bani Hassan. You know, I'm somebody!' Even though he's walking on the road. Whereas in Lebanon I can't imagine that would happen. What would be the equivalent? What would give somebody honor if they were seen as poor and walking on the roadside like a laborer? Without a car. But for him, his identity was in something a bit different than in purely what job he did and how much money he had. I think because almost everyone is connected to the rural roots—even Palestinian Jordanians—everyone knows they're from this village, and that gives them an identity."

Prior to 2003 pretension was virtually unknown in Iraq, according to Amjad, but since the war, people have changed somewhat. A rich person might build an "unnaturally huge" house, or the middle class person might park his "extravagant car" in front of his modest home. However, for the vast majority of people, a simple, decent home is enough. Iraqis in general are not particularly class-conscious.

Maryam, from a well-known clan in Yemen, described the importance of image:

> In my family, sometimes there wasn't any money after my father died. But mother would struggle for us to live at the level people knew us to be in. Maybe there wouldn't be food and drink in the house, but we had to have a pool—the best,

and go to the best schools. So that's how it is for my family and my social class. But for the rest of the people, no. They are simple people, good people who present good hospitality, but they live naturally.

Wade agreed that the majority of the Yemeni people are poor and, although they generally try to dress nicely like others, aren't trying to show off. However, the middle class is more tempted to value appearances, and a car—even one that barely runs—is a big status symbol. There are a few occasions during which people of all standards seek to make a dazzling impression, such as weddings, births, and *sublit al-eid*.[475] At these times, the cost of meeting and exceeding cultural norms of hospitality can devastate a family financially. In fact, it is not unusual in several countries in the region for families to go into debt to finance weddings and hospitality.

Eva was proud to have grown up in a household in which no guest who entered would have realized that her father was a blue-collar worker. Glades talked about people in Aleppo who would go into debt to hide the fact that they were in penury, but "the *qirsh* [small coin] they get is a source of pain for them," perpetuating the cycle of poverty.

Look at me, world!

The interviewees I asked all said without doubt that many Lebanese pretend to have more than they actually have. Elias told me:

> Ninety percent of the Lebanese . . . are concerned with the external situation. They buy a car, the latest model. You enter their house. The living room is very good, but the bedrooms are not good enough by any means. People don't see the bedrooms. "Look at me, world!"

---

[475] Literally, "the tail of the feast." This phrase refers to the days following the official days off, which Yemenis make a practice of turning into an extended holiday.

Appearances in Lebanon
- Abu Nader gave the example of someone who makes $135 per month and spends $30 or $40 one weekend on a rental car which he pretends to own.
- A student told me a few years ago of a young man who caused an accident while speeding through an intersection driving a black Mercedes and talking on the phone. Police found the body of the unregistered car to be thoroughly rusted, but carefully patched with cardboard, taped and painted. The car motor was an elderly Toyota engine, and the cell phone turned out to be a $1 children's toy.
- Zeina described people going into debt to buy the best clothes. She liked the practice in most Lebanese schools of wearing uniforms because it eases the pressure on children and teens to keep up appearances. For Zeina, part of godly parenting is to teach children the right balance in their choice of clothes.
- Many young people choose their profession based on prestige. Marwan was pleased to be going into business, even though it doesn't have the image, because at least there will be work. Of his classmates he said, "All of them want to become a doctor, a lawyer or an engineer, but there are too many of them in Lebanon."
- Marwan: "I know someone who goes to a restaurant, and if he has someone with him, might pay $30 just to drink this bottle of whiskey. Or, never mind, he throws things away unopened or lights them on fire."
- Rana: "As soon as I arrive at a place, I see my friends sitting, and everyone is dressed chicly, and each one has his own cell phone, and so on. And I say, 'O God! Do I really want to go in among them?' Even though my father owns a business. All of the Lebanese people are like that—it's all they talk about. Appearance is more important to them than anything."

> • "They give the impression to the world that they have so that no one looks on them and says, 'Those poor people are without.' They won't accept people saying that of them. From the outside they appear to be rich, but inside they haven't got a morsel to eat. No one can show them kindness and say, 'Eat!' They get upset. They show self-respect. They want to work." (Eva, a Syrian living in Lebanon)

What drives some to behave this way? My interviewees each had their own explanations. Marwan said they want to draw attention to themselves. Bemoaning the fact that many Lebanese put themselves into debt to imitate the lifestyles of others, Louisa chalked it up to lack of acceptance of their situation or financial status. Nayla speculated,

> Sometimes prestige . . . Sometimes appearances . . . Sometimes he feels ashamed, he has no self-confidence. He doesn't want it to show . . . He doesn't want society to look down on him. Sometimes it's ignorance.

Zeina offered a similar blend of reasons:

> Because maybe they are jealous of someone. So that no one will say to them, "Look what you're wearing! How can you wear such a thing? What a pity that you dress like that!" No, they wear expensive things so they can say, "Look, I'm dressed like them." They are not content with their life. The one who is content with his life lives very happily.

In Ram's opinion, showing off wealth is a matter of gaining respect: "If I have money, but walk in simplicity and it doesn't show, the people will not treat me with respect. If I dress well, they're going to respect me very much." Fouad reported that a number of people reside in the grounds of his church in Sudan because it gives them a more respectable address that they would have if they continued to live with their families.

Abu Nader believed that people who feign wealth are trying to escape from the painful truth of the situation in which they live, but Elias is less sympathetic:

Elias: Because they love appearances. They love—maybe they will be a simple employee—but they like to show off to the neighbors, "Look at me!" And this is against the Christian religion, and also against the Islamic religion, for sure. But regrettably, Lebanon is living this way.
Karen: The person who does this, what is in his heart, what does he desire from this?
Elias: The desire is love of self.
Karen: But it's as though he *doesn't* love himself.
Elias: He doesn't love others, he loves himself. He loves appearances. He loves to wear the most expensive label clothing.

Marwan told me that the way others view this spendthrift behavior varies, depending on whether "there is personal advantage or if there is not. If there is personal advantage, 'Yeah, let's go!' They go along with him regardless of how right or wrong he is. They want something from him. And the one who doesn't want something, 'What is this ignorant person?!'"

The interviewees also expressed concern that social and economic pretenses have political and religious ramifications. Zeina claimed that "a lot of politicians are criminals—but it doesn't show." Abu Nader had little regard for politicians who attend weddings and funerals and pretend to care, but their real hope is getting votes. Once again, men of religion came in for considerable criticism for false faith, false vocations, and pretentious lifestyles. Ahmad said of the clergy:

> . . . all the world is hiding behind one finger. They all say, "I'm pious," and then you find that they are doing something illicit and contrary. Those are a bunch of upstarts. What matters to them is

that they get to a certain goal. We wish that the piety would be a true piety. . . .

Louisa, whose religious community maintains distinctive clothing for the varying ranks of religious seniority, made clear that piety has not the least thing to do with whether or not one wears religious dress:

> It's not the dress, it's what you are inside. If you are a believer, I think there will be something shining here in your heart. But it's not the dress, the scarf, the turban, or whatever they wear. It's related to the person himself, so there is no difference whether he is a religious man by appearance or religious lady, and if he's pious or not.

The public fasting of some Muslims made Charlie cynical:

> When it comes to Ramadan, when they are supposed to be more inclined toward prayer, inclined more toward charitable reactions to people, not just charity itself, it's the worst time of the year to get into an argument with a Muslim. Inadvertently, he'll bring up the fact that he is fasting and you have to give him that extra space to get angry or react negatively because he is hungry and he is trying to curb his . . . Well, come on! I don't know if God wants us to fast with that kind of attitude, you know? And when you look at what Jesus had to say about fasting . . . Between you and God. Only.

Nayla's concern was the impeachment of Christian witness that results from leaders who love appearances:

> I've seen priests . . . Sometimes I sense, even among us [Evangelicals], a lot of appearances, you know, appearances of wealth, that give the impression to the non-Christians about them, as though those big in religion are not Christians. How can I put it? Even my [Muslim] son the other day said, "'Look at the Patriarch, how he's dressed." It wasn't gold but all of it points to exorbitant wealth. And among the people, "Where does it come from? From where? From where?"

Coming to Beirut from the West Bank, Ram shared the same concern about the obsession with appearances he has seen among lay Christians in Lebanon. He was alarmed at the degree to which they value prestige—more, in his opinion, than do most Muslims.

Abu Nader saw the temptation to love appearance as a spiritual challenge for everyone, for many feign piety just as many feign wealth or hardship.

Abu Nader: If I worship God, to whom am I praying or fasting? To whom?
Karen: To God!
Abu Nader: To God. You don't force me. I do it for God. I don't fast so that you can see how pious I am. In my work, in my daily practice, in my daily labor, with my wife, my children, with you, with the neighbors, that is piety. If I see someone poor . . . I have to help them. That is piety. Piety is not habitual, that every day I take the prayer beads and pray and grow a beard and become a sheikh or become a priest—this is not piety. This is appearance, appearances. Piety is that a person is pious within himself. His heart—that is the foundation. When I pray to God I don't want all the world saying, "Look! That one is praying." No. Maybe I will stay in a place in which no one sees me. No one sees me? God sees me. I am praying to God. I don't want the world to see me. What has the world got to do with it?

For Charlie, the absence of the need to impress others is a sign of spiritual maturity. He explained:

> People are empty. They're looking for something to fill that gap, and that's why in the lives of true Christians, pious, truly pious Christians, they don't care about these things. I don't need to impress anybody. That emptiness is filled with the Lord. I'm totally full. There's nothing lacking in my soul that I need to fill with external riches, or to impress. And here's another thing: You notice in the lives of Christians that that interest [in impressing others] is inversely proportional to their level of spirituality. Underline inversely.

It seems that, in Middle Eastern thinking, the issue of appearance is not seen particularly as an issue of right and wrong. On the large survey I conducted, four school students credit their good rich acquaintances with not flaunting or showing off their wealth. Otherwise the surveys have nothing to say on the matter, good or bad. However, the school sample also indicated that the young people are very conscious of the symbols of wealth and class status around them. Cars and/or houses were mentioned by over half of the students, sometimes with details: the number of cars, the model or year of car, the number of rooms in the house, and so on. Several also noted lavish spending patterns, clothes or jewelry, and associations with wealthy countries.

Middle Easterners have an ambiguous relationship with image.[476] While poverty is an embarrassment, being clever enough to exploit the sympathy of the naïve is seen by some as admirable, or at least profitable enough to risk a blush. It is very difficult to attain any position of influence in the social, religious, or political circles of the Middle East without the trappings of wealth and prestige, and the pressures are intense to be ostentatious in dress, driving, dining, and dwelling. And yet these symbols of prestige which lift a person to success rob him of respect: self-respect and the respect of lower- and middle-class fellow-citizens. People may admire, envy, and imitate the pretentious, but they do not esteem them in their hearts. It follows, then, that it is very hard to be perceived as both righteous and rich, for the righteous do not live for appearances, deny reality, or scorn those with less, but generally in the Middle East, the rich do.

Appearances and the Bible
Solomon was famous for his flamboyance. In one sense, the grandeur of his kingdom brought glory to the Lord because of the temple the king built and dedicated to God. However, the splendor described in 1 Kings 10 was both enhanced and polluted by his marriages to pagan royalty described in 1 Kings 11; marriages which caused the

---

[476] For an article by a Lebanese on "love" of appearances, see "One Midsummer Day and Night" by Nahla Atiyah, http://www.dailystar.com.lb/Nahla-Atiyah.ashx.

Almighty to work against Solomon. Nevertheless, this is probably the most positive biblical account of a love of appearances.

In Deuteronomy, God forbids even royalty from presumption and an attitude of superiority.[477] Hezekiah's ostentatious display of wealth doomed his royal household.[478] The prophets have no time for pretentious homes and costumes.[479] In 1 Timothy, wealthy women are commanded to dress simply and modestly, as appropriate for women professing godliness.[480] And Jesus pulled no punches when condemning those who allow their love of appearances to infect their piety.[481] Seeking to gain human approval, according to Paul, means that one has ceased to serve God.[482] Love of appearances is one area in which the Word of God stands in judgment of a common cultural tendency in Lebanon, and to a lesser degree, in other parts of the Middle East.

Pretend poverty isn't much addressed in the Bible, but the motivations my interviewees posited for it are. Discontent, grumbling, and envy are condemned throughout the Scriptures as a sign of rebellion against the sovereign will of God.[483] The Proverbs eschew all forms of deceit in order to take advantage.[484] Paul condemns as "worse than an infidel" the person capable of caring for his or her family who allows the church to support them.[485] Ananias and Sapphira paid a fearful price for pretending to be poorer than they were in order to give less.[486] The opposites of all these things are elevated in the Bible: contentment, gratitude and praise, wanting others to get ahead, generosity, and financial responsibility.

---

[477] Deuteronomy 17:14–20.
[478] Isaiah 39 and parallels.
[479] Isaiah 3:16–4:1; Amos 6:4–7.
[480] 1 Timothy 2:9,10. Cf. 1 Peter 3:3,4.
[481] Matthew 6:1–6; 23:5–12.
[482] Galatians 1:10; 1 Thessalonians 2:5.
[483] Deuteronomy 5:21; Deuteronomy 1:19–31; Psalm 106:24–26; Ecclesiastes 4:8; Philippians 2:14.
[484] Proverbs 10:9; 12:22; 30:8,9.
[485] 1 Timothy 5:8,16 (KJV).
[486] Acts 5:1–11.

Appearances in Practice

We will not win people to Christ by impressing them with our clothes, but with our lives.[487] Few foreign Christians in the Middle East drive Mercedes Benz cars or wear $900 dresses imported from Paris and Rome. The casual lifestyle many Westerners maintain in the Middle East is a welcome change to Middle Easterners longing for simplicity and sincerity. Since imitating the West is a popular sport in many parts of the Middle East, Western followers of Jesus can have a positive influence in the society and the church by modeling simplicity as a viable alternative to the economically suicidal game of keeping up with the Haddads.

However, several words of caution are in order. While missionary fashions and furniture tend to be less pretentious than that of Middle Easterners, there are some things workers do which seem very show-offish, such as owning large four-wheel-drive vehicles, frequent travel to prosperous nations, and educating our children in the best schools. One must be careful to appear to live at a level consistent with one's means. Christine Mallouhi gives a negative example of a young couple of language students who moved into an up-scale neighborhood and straightaway furnished their entire apartment with new furniture, inviting gossip and speculation by the neighbors.[488] It is wise for us to have an idea of how our choices are perceived by those to whom we witness. If our lifestyles inspire envy, greed, inferiority, resentment, or self-destructive imitation, we may be undermining the ministry to which we have been called.

What we see as simple may be viewed as gauche or eccentric. A braided pony-tail on a 30-year-old woman in America might be considered down-to-earth: in the Middle East, it's from another planet altogether. Wearing faded jeans to Sunday worship in some Western settings shows comfort and familiarity—in many Middle Eastern churches it shows contempt. If you wish to model simplicity to Middle Eastern people, you must model simplicity *as the Middle Eastern people understand it*. The goal is not to import Western styles

---

[487] Richard Foster, *Celebration of Discipline: The Path to Spiritual Growth* (New York: Harper & Row, 1978), 79.
[488] The story is found in Christine A. Mallouhi, *Miniskirts, Mothers & Muslims: A Christian Woman in a Muslim Land.* (Oxford: Monarch, 2004), 38.

and values, but to adopt biblical principles in a culturally appropriate manner.[489]

Because appearances are so important in Middle Eastern society, some things which we see as honorable are considered humiliating by Middle Easterners and others in the region. For example, the manual labor which is considered "good, honest, hard work" in the West is looked down upon in much of the Arab world, as are the people who do the work.[490] Disabled people who try to live a normal, public life in society are seen by some Middle Easterners as shaming their families by letting it be seen that there is an abnormality in the home. Expatriates should be sensitive and discreet to avoid causing loss of face, especially for those already on the underside of life. Also, foreign workers should not assume that their own actions will be judged by Western standards of honor. If ordinary Middle Eastern people see someone picking up litter off the sidewalk and throwing it away, they will not think, "How tidy and community conscious that person is!" They will think, "There's a person without a shred of self-respect!"

It can be very costly in Middle Eastern society to drop out of the appearances rat race (or to refuse to enter it). Workers must weigh up whether their lifestyle choices will cut them off completely from those to whom they wish to share Christ, or from those upon whom they are dependent to carry on their ministry. Conversations with senior church leaders have made me aware that workers who have chosen to live modestly are both a source of great embarrassment and a cause of longing to those who would like to escape the appearances trap, but find they cannot.

Just because some Western religious workers have more modest cars, clothes, and houses than their local associates, it does not necessarily follow that these workers are poorer or perceived as being poorer. Middle Eastern people are aware that there are those who hide their wealth for less-than-noble motives. While it is a scriptural imperative that we not show off what we have, it is also important that we not try to conceal the blessings God has given us, especially

---

[489] There is an excellent chapter devoted to perceptions of furnishings, clothing and jewelry in the Arab world in Mallouhi, *Miniskirts*, chapter 2 "Living with Status," 35–51.
[490] Mallouhi, *Miniskirts*, 17–18.

if our concealment is a symptom of unwillingness to share or a lack of contentment. Openhandedness is just as much an imperative of Scripture as simplicity.

On the other hand, the slightly more closed hand, I heard warnings from Syria, Lebanon, Palestine, and Sudan about how frequently foreign aid money is given with good intentions but bad judgment to people who exploit the ignorance of the foreign donors and aid organizations. The interviewees repeatedly warned that you can't believe every story you hear, and that often those who cry the loudest and most convincingly are not what they appear. Seeking guidance from a variety of trusted sources can help, as can maintaining higher levels of accountability than are the norm in this part of the world.

There is a big difference between unchosen poverty and chosen poverty.[491] One of the dangers of an incarnational model for determining missionary lifestyles among the poor is that it may lead us to pretend that we are something we are not.[492] Middle Easterners as a rule are very skilled at detecting deception in another person, even if that other is self-deceived about his or her level of wealth. Western workers have, to quote Ahmad, "rich connections" and could leave a life of poverty to escape war or procure a life-saving operation for a son or daughter. Further, we are not normally saddled to the same degree with the financial expectations of family and relations. Even if workers were to choose to live at exactly the level of the people around, those workers would be insulting the neighbors if they claimed to be sharing fully in the local predicament. It would also be lacking in integrity, and as Daoud said, "Integrity is the most important thing." Sober consideration of our real assets in a Middle-Eastern ministry context may require that we revise our economic self-perception.

Although dealt with in more detail elsewhere, it is worth mentioning here also that a choice to live and work among the

---

[491] Jeff Hann, in a personal e-mail correspondence, 2001, reported by Ken Baker in "The Incarnational Model: Perception of Deception?" (*Evangelical Missions Quarterly*, 38:1, January 2002), 20.

[492] Harriet Hill, "Incarnational Ministry: A Critical Examination" (*Evangelical Missions Quarterly*, 26, April 1990), 196–203, found in Ken Baker. "The Incarnational Model: Perception of Deception?" (*Evangelical Missions Quarterly*, 38:1, January 2002), 20.

very poor is unlikely to be understood or appreciated by Middle Easterners.[493] Even the choices like using public transport[494] or driving an old car will knock a person down several pegs in the opinions of many Middle Easterners. When it comes to the issue of appearances, one walks a tightrope between conforming to the world's standards and avoiding unnecessary offense.

This can become paralyzing. Therefore, I end this chapter with the best advice on the subject, which comes from Charlie:

> People are going to talk. No matter what you do, okay? Well, let them talk! Don't give them a listening ear. If you've done something wrong, those who care about you are not going to talk in public. They're going to come to you and say, "In this cultural context, this is how we do things." And you will be more than willing to listen, because they cared to give you constructive criticism. But for people to sit publicly and, you know, blabbing their mouths against you, how you have failed culturally to serve a proper meal, these people don't care about you. They just want to be critical. So that's why I tell missionaries, "Don't listen!" If you know God approves, and you have done to the best of your ability, and you have sought counsel, especially in certain areas on what to do, and you are trying to follow that counsel to the best of your ability, don't listen. People are going to talk.

---

[493] Greg Livingstone gives examples and explanations of this difficulty of living among the poor in his book *Planting Churches in Muslim Cities*, 89–90.

[494] For a similar example in Cairo, see Mallouhi, *Miniskirts*, 28.

8

Friendship between Rich and Poor

Can there be true friendship between rich and poor? The consensus: yes, in theory, but almost never in practice. Interviewees from the middle class were notably more optimistic about the possibility than those from the lower class. Repeatedly, I asked the question and received affirmative answers which ranged from a definitive yes to a grudging admission that it *might* be possible *under certain conditions*. However, when asked to tell about a friendship they were familiar with between people of diverse economic standards, nearly all of the interviewees either drew a blank, described a patronage relationship,[495] or did the opposite and told about a relationship destroyed by the money barrier. A variety of metaphors described the same thought, that even in the best of circumstances, a rich-poor friendship would have "distance," "a wall," "a gap," "a barrier," "a crack." Christine Mallouhi claims that this class separation is practiced across the Muslim world. She writes, " . . . the basis for not living across diverse classes in Muslim culture is simply pragmatic. The culture will not allow you to do it."[496]

Barriers to Friendship between Poor and Rich

Marwan explained that friendship is built on mutual activities and exchange. For example, if a rich friend wants to go out, the poor person has a choice between not going, allowing the rich friend to pay, or ruining himself by going. None of these options will enhance the relationship. Nayla took up the same idea:

---
[495] The next chapter is all about patronage relationships.
[496] Mallouhi, *Miniskirts*, 27.

They would be different in how they spend their free time and their outings. The rich have an outing and the poor can't go. It is hard for rich and poor to be friends. Very hard. Such a friendship will not grow.... The rich person always gets on better with the rich. Maybe the poor person gets on better with the poor. They understand how they think, they understand how they live. They have many shared things between them. Always there is a big difference.

Nayla was sensitive to class distinctions in her church. She noticed a difference between the way prosperous members greet one another and the way they greet her. She does not believe this to be an intentional slight so much as an expression of the fact that rich people feel more comfortable with rich people. But it does make it hard for the less privileged to belong fully:

> It took me a long time to find my place in the church. I did it by my own effort, conquering my shyness and embarrassment, encouraging myself that in Christ I am not inferior to others. Maybe the poor always will feel different than the rich.

The rich, I was told repeatedly, simply do not associate with the poor, or even with the middle class. According to Zeina, the very rich "do not love people.... They don't talk to people who are not like themselves. They don't mix with them.... You won't find anyone from the middle class who is able to live with them." Social snobbery is inculcated into the children so that middle-class children are socially excluded at elite schools, Zeina claims. She found the rich person "who has no free time and doesn't talk to anyone" an especially doubtful prospect as a friend. Elias had similar complaints. He reported about some wealthy people he knows, " . . . they say with all candor, 'We don't have dinner except with people of our value, those who have money like us.' They fancy themselves above the middle class and poor class."

Elias believed that this class snobbery is the norm. Asked what would happen if a rich person visited his home, Elias speculated:

... if he didn't know me previously, I would assume that he is fancying himself at my expense. ... I would say, in principle, that the rich person wouldn't repeat the visit, especially here in Lebanon. The rich have dinner only with the rich. And this is something regrettable.

Most of the lower-class interviewees couldn't agree more. Doubting the prosperous person's potential for godliness, Nayla says:

He doesn't live with people who are lesser than himself, who have less. He stays only with people who are like himself. This is the barrier: he doesn't even see the people around him.

Abu Nader had very low expectations of the rich when it comes to befriending the poor:

Abu Nader: No. He wouldn't become his companion—wouldn't even greet him.
Karen: Just "hello," and that's it?
Abu Nader: Maybe not even that.

He also claimed that class distinction is a kind of power distance[497] which inhibits wholesome and lasting relationships. "Riches mean authority. Money means that between rich and poor there is not going to be friendship." He continued:

Okay, the poor person is going to look at the rich as though, well, he is living in a big house and I am living in a room. He rides in a car, and I haven't got a car. His children are in the best universities, and I can't educate my children. He sits at a big dining table, and I am not able to feed my children a dish of rice. It might be that the poor person would make a visit to the rich person, but will the rich

---

[497] "Power distance" measures the extent to which subordinates expect and accept that power is distributed unequally. In the relationship between leaders and followers "power distance" measures the extent to which a leader can determine the behavior of the follower, and the extent to which the follower can or cannot influence the leader. Geert Hofstede, *Cultures and Organizations: Software of the Mind* (London: McGraw-Hill, 1991), 28.

person visit the home of the poor?! There is no friendship. It's a form of authority: the rich over the poor. The interests would not be the interests of friendship.

A rich-poor friendship depends on the attitude of the wealthier partner, according to Zeina. She said, "You'll find friendship if the person is pious. The rich person, I mean." A wealthy Yemeni told me, "We don't look at the other classes or at people who work at lowly jobs. They are good people in our society, but it is hard to marry them." Ram told me, "No one remembers the poor," and it was generally accepted by all that some rich people do not want to be seen in the company of the poor for fear of losing prestige, as Ram put it: "If I am rich, what will the people who are rich like me think if they see me interacting with someone like you?" Some of the affluent, I was told, like to be fussed over and treated almost as royalty.

> **You'll find friendship if the person is pious. The rich person, I mean.**

Knowing One's Worth

Nayla hated the condescension of the wealthy. Her most heated statement came in response to my asking how she would feel if a particular wealthy person visited her home:

Nayla: How would I feel if he came to my house? (Long pause). I don't know what you think of me. Do you expect me to say that would be humble of him!? I don't think so. I don't sense that he's a whole lot better than me. It's not pride that I think this way, you know? It's not humility on his part to visit.
Karen: Would you feel embarrassed?
Nayla: NO! Never. I would never feel ashamed. I know my worth!

> **Karen:** And your worth has nothing to do with money?
> **Nayla:** Nothing to do with money. I have worth as a person. Not in my house, not in my furnishings, not in . . . No. I know there are personalities that feel that way, that someone is really humbling himself to visit their home, but no, I have none of these feelings.

Since Abu Nader considered all men of religion rich, it is not surprising that they came in for special criticism as potential friends. Their wealth and the resentment it breeds in the heart of the have-nots is a barrier to relationship that no truly pious man would allow. As Abu Nader put it:

> . . . when I want to go and visit them, this sheikh (or this priest) who has hired a workman, and he has the best apartment, and he has the best car, how am I to feel? I labor for my money. My wife has to go to the market and buy her food—there is no workman to bring her groceries to her. And I don't ride in a car. The world doesn't ride in a car. If I am pious, if I am a sheikh, I don't want to. God doesn't tell me to do this. Likewise, if I were a priest. It shouldn't be like this. Christ wasn't like this.

Abu Nader found it particularly offensive that a sheikh would expect ordinary people to kiss his hand. When I ask Abu Nader at what level a man of religion should live, he was ready with an answer, "At the level of the people. At the level of love. At the level of piety."

The attitudes of the poor are also to blame, particularly in the eyes of the better-off interviewees. The poor are aware of the attitudes of the wealthy, Sayyid told me, and so are reluctant to pursue a close relationship for fear of rejection or embarrassment:

> If there is a rich man and I want to go on a trip, no. I'm going to find someone from my class and he and I will go on the trip. I'm not going to take Rabia with me, for example, because he might say, "This trip is not a good one. How are the people going to look

at me?" Maybe they will see one another, hug one another, visit one another on special occasions, but there is still this conservativism, this barrier.

According to Ram, the poor complain a lot, and they envy, badmouth, and have a negative view of the rich. "They think, 'We're better than him, even though he is rich.'" Fou'ad told a similar story:

> Poor or middle-class, they find barriers between themselves and the rich. They see themselves as simple. So without sensing it, he [the poor person] makes a barrier between himself and the rich. Because he has psychological weaknesses, he says, "The rich person looks at me that I am poor and when he interacts with me, he treats me with inferiority. So it is better to keep far from him so that I don't lower myself before him." And there are people who love the friendship because he lifts his head at the expense of the rich person. The motivation of the majority is that they have some emotional illness. They're not accepting their situation. I've seen many of my friends that have this sickness.

Ramy provided "another reason from the starting point of shame and honor," that the stigma of being thought of as an opportunist and social climber will cause the poor to distance himself. Ahmad thought the poor person should be reluctant to ask for or accept help, or the relationship might be destroyed. Likewise, Zeina said that the poorer partner must not be greedy or maintain the friendship only when it is profitable. She urged mutual giving and gratitude, even if the value of the gift is unequal:

> It is appropriate that the poor person gives to his rich friend whatever he can. Even if it's just that he has a garden, and he takes a rose and presents it to him. And the friend says, "Thank you. This is very good."

Ahmad had no hesitation whatever when asked if such a friendship is possible: "Of course!" He made a clear distinction between friendship and patronage, strongly implying that patronage and friendship are incompatible. Nearly everyone else, however, assumed that a subtle patronage would pervade any friendship between economic unequals. For example, Wade found that friends loaning friends money, a common occurrence in Yemen, impaired the mutuality of comradery. The Syrians I talked to assumed that if a poor person initiated a visit to someone well-off, people would think he was going because of need. Sayyid suggested that the rich person bring no gift, lest a gift turn the less financially fortunate recipient from respecting to using his upscale friends.

Expectations can even separate family members at different economic levels. Elias had relatives who would not dine with him because he was too poor. Maryam's mother moved away from her supportive family because she couldn't stand being the recipient of their constant and well-intentioned charity. Emad expressed sadness that he rarely saw his cousins as a child because, when his aunt's family visited, they brought gifts so generous that Emad's family were unable to reciprocate. To prevent embarrassment, his father limited their return visits to one financially devastating occurrence per year.

Possibilities of Friendship

Maryam felt that, throughout the region, friendship between people of different economic levels, although still very difficult, has become easier in recent years due to three factors: universities, more open social exchange, and the "Arab Spring" with its focus on democratization. Three people suggested special circumstances which would make easier the rare feat of maintaining interclass familiarity: an affection formed before the friends' statuses diverged, a business man whose job makes it natural for him to mix with others, and the context of the church. This last suggestion was made in a group interview with several evangelicals, most of whom disagreed: "They might go on a church trip together, but family friendship is rarely seen."

Piety on the part of both rich and poor would go a long way toward bridging that gap, according to Rana. Each one realizes that the other is not indebted to him, that his wealth or poverty is his own burden and responsibility, and that the visitor must share without reserve or guilt in what the host offers. In fact, a number of the interviewees pointed out the importance of the rich receiving hospitality from the poor. Lara said, "It's hospitality as equals. When we visit their shanties we expect something. It changes the power dynamic." That is, we become people who need something from the poor, who are indebted to the poor, and they become people with something to offer, people with honor. This requires the poor to overcome their embarrassment at the simplicity of their homes and food and to take the risk of inviting a wealthier person in.

What the Poor Want from the Rich

On no other topic were the interviewees more unanimous than when answering the question, "What do the poor want from the rich?" All answered, "Respect!" For most, it was the first word. For some, it was the only word, the word that said it all.

Respect is the bottom line. To this bare minimum of what the poor person desires, others added that

'What do the poor want from the rich?' All answered, 'Respect!' For most, it was the first word. For some, it was the only word, the word that said it all.

- the rich one doesn't let the poor person feel his poverty,
- he sets him at ease,
- he should be a friend who doesn't wait for groveling thanks—he is a friend because he wants to be, not as a service, and
- he accepts me as I am: I don't have to be like him, to reflect him, to eat in his way.

There is angst in Abu Nader's longing for a mutual interclass relationship:

Friendship. I might try it if I were rich. I'd take off my garment that speaks of money and go to your house, and we'd sit together, you and I, and eat from the same plate. That is friendship. Or if you're sick I look after you, but if one is poor and sick, would the other come and look after him? He forgets him. He forgets. He doesn't go to him.

> **Rich Friends or Rich Patrons**
> In addition to piety, the middle-class interviewees mentioned the characteristics listed below of an affluent friend in relation to a poor one. Some of these attributes stand on the blurred line between friendship and patronage.
> - is humble
> - has a kind heart
> - feels with people
> - asks, "How are you? How can I help you?"
> - moves closer when the lower-class friend is squeezed
> - gives clothes when they are needed
> - makes the life of the poor more comfortable
> - behaves normally and naturally
> - visits the down-and-out friend out of pity (note the contradiction with the previous entry)
> - dines together with the poor
> - repeats visits
> - is wise in giving help
> - welcomes the poor

Friendship between rich and poor in the Middle East is rarely more than a pipe dream. To minimize the gap, the truly pious person of any class will work hard to reduce attitudes of superiority or inferiority, strive to maintain fellow-feeling with people of another status, love people rather than use them, and show sincere, practical concern for an acquaintance in need. Whether this is foundation enough for a friendship remains in doubt.

The Bible and Friendship Between Rich and Poor

"A friend loves at all times," God tells us in the Proverbs.[498] The teachings of Christ and the exhortations of the epistles of the New Testament call for the sort of genuine love, humility, patience, and self-giving that make friendship possible.[499] But nowhere to my knowledge does the Word of God *require* friendship of the rich for the poor.

What is clearly required is to associate with the lowly, considering them brothers and sisters, not discriminating against them, treating them with respect, dining with them, and meeting their needs. In this, if the interviewees are right, many people in the region have a great deal to learn of what God requires.

Friendship in Practice

Pastor Charlie observed to me that many foreign Christians had little impact in the Middle East with people at any economic level because their work orientation and introversion kept them aloof:

> They need to be much more involved in the life of the community, the body. Be involved in a church. You need to be part of the local body. When you're part of the body, that not only involves you in the life of the church as a spiritual body, but also as a social body. Being involved in hospitality and generosity expands your horizon to reach people beyond the walls of the church.

It is generally unrealistic in the Middle East to try to maintain a variety of close friendships at significantly differing social strata. "If you aren't like the person, you won't become friends," Zeina advised. Workers living at any level of society will find themselves divided from some Middle Easterners by what Jonathan Bonk calls "an unbridgeable social gulf."[500] It makes sense to gear one's lifestyle to one's vocation, particularly if that vocation involves personal work

---

[498] Proverbs 17:17.
[499] For example, Matthew 7:12 and Colossians 3:12–14.
[500] In *Mission and Money* (Maryknoll: Orbis, 1991), 48–50. My failure to gain an interview with a very rich person is a cogent example.

such as friendship evangelism or personal discipleship. It is easiest, naturally, for the missionary to slip into the bracket of society which most resembles his or her home status, and this may prove the most fruitful level of ministry.

However, it is a matter of great concern if, in the overall choices of missionaries, certain segments of society are neglected, such as the very rich and the very poor. A friend serving among the poorest in Lebanon complains to me that she can always get donations from the expatriate Christian community, but not co-workers. It is comfortable for many Western expatriates to mix with the upper middle class and turn a blind eye to the thousands of poor. Yet God is not blind to them. Financing an effective ministry among the elite would be quite a challenge, but these are also in need of God's message of grace and freedom.

It concerns me that the middle-class interviewees were notably more optimistic about friendship between rich and poor than are their lower-class counterparts. Could it be that even the middle class, because they lack experience of extreme social distance, are unable to see through the eyes of the poor? Those doing ministry among the poor need to begin by listening, long and hard, preferably in people's homes over glasses of tea. Particularly when dining in the homes of the disadvantaged, it would be well to heed Jesus' injunction that his disciples should eat whatever is set before them.[501]

It may be hard for Westerners who value the concept of equal opportunity to limit their focus to one class or sub-class, especially considering the fact that such a focus will likely be further narrowed by constraints of ethnic, tribal, or religious divisions. However, public ministries allow greater diversity. In this, Jesus is an example. He ministered to wealthy centurions and destitute widows, but made his working-class disciples the focus of his efforts.

I have been told from time to time by middle-class Syrians and Lebanese that I should not be mixing with specific poor acquaintances. Some close friends once even threatened not to allow their children to play in our home any more if we continued to receive the children of the Bedouin concierge down the street. I've

---

[501] Luke 10:8.

chosen to use these occasions to point to the teachings of Jesus rather than to conform to the culture. If we snub the poor for the sake of our witness to Christ, I wonder to what Christ we are witnessing. By the way, despite the threat, the children returned after we explained our reasons for receiving Bedouin children and our unwillingness to stop, and no further comment was made.

Although it is expedient to have a focus in terms of economic level, it is also imperative to show love to all people. Love in this cultural context means visiting people's homes, speaking to them normally, not being ashamed of them, and listening eagerly to their stories and perspectives. It also means offering practical care when there is need. My own experience is that genuine words of kindness, respectful treatment, and being willing to be seen in public with the person go a long way toward securing a wholesome relationship.[502]

In relating to those of a higher status, the worker should be sure that he or she genuinely cares for the person and is not merely trying to solicit funds or exploit advantageous connections, however noble the cause. It is also worth remembering how important appearances are, and to avoid being an embarrassment through inappropriate manners, dress, choice of restaurant, and the like.

---

[502] More will be said on the matter in the discussion of patronage in the next chapter.

9

Patrons and Clients

An Introduction to the Patron-Client Relationship[503]

Let's start with a definition of the concept of patrons and clients:

> Patron-client relations are social relationships between individuals based on a strong element of inequality and difference in power. The basic structure of the relationship is an exchange of different and very unequal resources. A patron has social, economic, and political resources that are needed by a client. In return, a client can give expressions of loyalty and honor that are useful for the patron.[504]

Patronage permeates the social and economic structure of countries throughout the region. One author describes how patronage works in many countries around the world:

> Gifts are a means of buying loyalty and service. Gifts mitigate an unjust and harsh social system. People are honored to have a patron, a protector. A person may be exploited, but he

---

[503] I am grateful to Dr. Diane King, formerly of the American University of Beirut, for drawing my attention to the patron-client relationship as the best construct for explaining many of the comments in the interviews.

[504] Kawtharani, Farah Wajih. "The Interplay of Clientelism and Ethnic Identity in Pluralist States: The Case of the Kurdish Community in Lebanon." Unpublished MA thesis, American University of Beirut, 2003. I am relying a great deal on chapters 2 and 4 of this work. I have confidence in her findings because fifteen years of strange and frustrating experiences in Syria and Lebanon suddenly made sense when I read them.

or she is also protected by the "father." Patronage is a normal feature of shame-based, hierarchical societies.[505]

Patronage permeates Middle Eastern life. The political system is infused with it, but it also functions in most organizations and institutions, families, places of worship, and even interpersonal relationships. Families function as patrons to their members, and young people are hard-pressed to find work or get married unless the family is confident of their loyalty. This makes being a believer in Christ from a Muslim background especially difficult, for the convert is often seen as ungrateful and disloyal. It is not unusual for a MBB to give up the faith and return to his family to find work and escape destitution.

Patronage has been around for a long time in this part of the world. Prior to the advent of the modern nation-state, feudal lords governed much of the Middle East. These lords did not exercise their authority by force alone. Rather, they knew the people under their jurisdiction, and earned and maintained the loyalty of the people by providing them with protection, relief in times of disaster, and services. The system relied on mutual obligations and exchange. This pattern of patronage and clientelism infiltrated the modern nation-state structure which was imposed upon it. Politicians, senior clergy and, in some countries, royalty play the role of lords who used their positions to the personal advantage of those under their authority, and in return expected loyalty and support for their ambitions. They use their political clout to ensure that their supporters are provided with protection and services, making use of loyal bureaucrats who expect promotions and favors. Ordinary citizens promote the election of their patron to office and do what they can to further him in his career, knowing that his success means benefits for them.

One of the most important services that patrons perform is in taking the role of the *wasīṭ*, or providing *wasṭa*. Wasṭa is the expenditure of one's influence on behalf of another person. The wasīṭ, or go-between, might help the client get a job or weasel out of a traffic fine, speak as an informal advocate for the client in a dispute,

---

[505] Lingenfelter, *Transforming Culture*, 94–97.

introduce the client to a senior person, hurry along a document stalled in a bureaucratic jam, or any number of other services. While most of these favors do not cost the wasīṭ money, they do cost in the social bank of one-hand-washing-the-other. So the client finds ways to repay this societal debt with a well-placed vote or word of praise, with a return favor, by ignoring a fault, or making a donation, for example.

> **Patronage and Wasṭa in Egypt**
> One needs many acquaintances to help make connections in Egypt because of its mammoth bureaucracy and vast population. This is how it was explained to me:
>
> **M:** If I want help from so-and-so, I need to know a person who can introduce me to so-and-so. Levels. Layers.
> **K:** So if N, for example, introduced you to someone big, do you have an obligation to her?
> **M:** Of course!
> **K:** What is this obligation?
> **M:** Sometimes it stays material, sometimes it is notional. For instance, if N stood by me today, then one day I stand beside her in some matter. And the material, that's obvious. If you want something that's a certain price, I get it done for you, and it's finished. Your solution.
> **E:** If N were to know someone big in a position of responsibility, I need another person to introduce me to N so that I can get to know this big person.
> **K:** We have a lot of this because we are a very large country with a lot of poverty. Merely helping the poor is an achievement, something big. So this happens a lot at election time. Before the elections, the politicians go down and do this in the villages. It's like oil.
> **E:** "Did you take the oil?" [All the Egyptians laughed heartily.]

The Relationship Between Patron and Client

In the course of the interviews, I heard the stories of clients and their attitudes toward their patrons. Maryam's family, although functioning as patrons to others, needed a patron to pay for long-term medical care:

> When my brother traveled to Bosnia, he was hit by a shell. One of the biggest sheikhs gave support to the injured youths, including my brother. He didn't ask anything, but my brother has big loyalty and big thanks to this sheikh who gave us support.

A Shi'ite passionately poured out this panegyric about Nasrallah, head of Hezbollah:

> You know who I am talking about. All the world knows him. All the world tries to blacken to you his qualities, and yet he is a provider for them. He is not killing them; he protects. He isn't grasping his weapons and his money, he isn't killing with them. He is protecting with them. He is walking with us in an Islamic way. We don't care what others think. Or what the nations think, or what the Sunnis think, or what the Shi'ites think—none of them. We are thinking from one perspective only: his perspective is our perspective. Not because he has weapons and money and we are following him—no. But only because he knows our Lord, because he is carrying his money, carrying his weapons, to defend us, not to go to war with the world. All of us are concerned for him; he's not spending for us [that is, not buying us], he's protecting us.

Although Elias used the world "friendship," it is clear that he was describing from his own experience the correct posture of the disadvantaged toward his patron:

> ... the poor, as soon as he sees the rich person helping him in a clever way, certainly, if he [the patron] needs him, will maybe give him his life, empty his life for him. This is the sweet friendship between the rich and the poor, because he senses that the rich

person is helping him indirectly, in a clever way. And in the circumstance that the rich person contacts him, and is in need of him or in a dangerous situation, the poor person is ready to sacrifice his life for him.

An Egyptian living in Lebanon gave this account:

I have a friend who had a problem with his heart and the operation cost thousands of dollars. He arrived at Saad al-Hariri, and he offered him assistance, and he went to the American hospital, and he did the operation. He paid some token amount. So if he weren't affiliated with this person, may God not permit it, he would have died. He would not have done the operation.

Zeina's relatives have benefited from al-Hariri's services:

My sister's hands hurt her. She went to the clinic, and they said, "A million lira." [Approximately US$67,000]. He enabled her to have an operation on her hands. They gave her money, and she gave them a report from the clinic of American University Hospital—never mind: She wanted to go to a smart doctor. My sister, her husband doesn't work, you see. Every year at Ramadan they send a package in which she finds pulses (seed/grain) and food and ghee and oil and the like. They send her a message: "Your things are here, come and get them." They distribute a lot. My sister's daughter studied nutrition at AUB. Her father was retrenched during the war. Hariri paid for her education. We saw with our own eyes. He helped her and he took no money from her. She now works and travels and goes out, and he doesn't take money from her.

The Late Rafik al-Hariri as Patron

My initial study of wealth and piety in 2005 nearly drowned at birth in the tidal wave of grief at the death of Lebanon's richest man and the passionate eulogies which were spoken in his behalf by ordinary people. I was on the verge of letting it slip under the waves, when I was advised, "Latch on to what they're saying, and you'll learn something about Middle Eastern society." I grasped, and found that I was clutching something rather more substantial than straw. Lebanon stays afloat by patronage, and the death of al-Hariri was the death of the man many considered Lebanon's greatest patron.

The positive qualities ascribed to the former Prime Minister were directly related to issues of patronage. Foremost is the assistance he gave to the poor and to students. Services mentioned include help given to the poor who asked for it, rebuilding Beirut after the war, furthering people in their careers, operating charitable foundations, providing scholarships, and opening a university.

Some added qualifying phrases confirming that he gave these services from genuine piety. For example:
- "He values intentions, and not money."
- "He showed humility."
- "He took on the donation of money as a good deed."
- ". . . despite that he had no need for a position."
- "He helped people in accordance with his pure intentions."
- "He is very kind, gives for others, a loving father."
- "He was a good person and helped others."

Some of the survey-takers noted that Hariri's services had been for the good of the whole country:
- "He took on many good deeds for the revitalization of his homeland, Lebanon."
- "He loved his homeland until martyrdom . . ."
- "Education, success, and faithfulness. He raised the country to new life. Educated the new generation."
- "He wanted the good and the best for Lebanon."
- "He did everything he could for Lebanon, helped Lebanon in times of crisis."
- "He rebuilt the country he loved."
- "He worked for the goodness of his country, society, and all Lebanese people, Muslims and Christians."

- "He helped the poor and did not distinguish between denominations."

The timing of my original study resulted in an inflated emphasis on Rafik al-Hariri as the preferred public image of a pious rich man. But al-Hariri was not the only patron Lebanese people mentioned. In fact, 122 of 141 explanations given in the survey for the choice of a well-known character who combines wealth and goodness fall neatly into the category of patronage. Patronage is considered a virtue of the righteous rich in the Middle East as a foundational value, and not merely as a temporary fad related to the death of a great political patron.

Advantages of Patronage

Government safety nets in the region tend to be knotted rather loosely, and the little people fall through with distressing regularity. Without patrons, they would be helpless. As Eva said, "Unless you find some good people that have humanity, who will help you?! It is impossible." She told of a well-off Lebanese who made all the difference for her family when they arrived as refugees from Syria, "He has . . . I'm not saying millions and millions, but he has money. He helps the poor. He has a good heart. He likes to help, I mean a lot, those around him. At the last minute, he was holding my husband's hand. If it weren't for him . . . !" Lara has worked with a whole community of people who have "come to the end and they need input quickly." Patrons are desperately needed.

This is not only true when it comes to material needs, but also true when a person needs special dispensation or help in peeling away red tape. Eva told with immense gratitude of a person who worked with her family to get their legal papers in order.

In rural areas or small towns, patronage can work well, according to some Egyptians. In the cities, the lack of personal relationship between the patron and the clients allows both parties to focus on money and power out of the context of the good of the whole. In a village, patrons know they will be held somewhat accountable since they have to live with their clients daily, and greedy clients cannot easily manipulate a patron by hiding their true financial ability.

Rana praised the righteous patron as a role model: "We act like him, we pray like him, we do everything like him. There are a lot of people, sheikhs, who have money and fear God." Patrons have the ear and loyalty of many, and therefore are able to influence public thinking. Marwan cited the positive example of a well-known Lebanese singer and actor:

> George Khabbaz certainly has a lot of money. But he always gives to the Lebanese people something they haven't got, that they don't know. For example, he did a film called "Gabi" on the people who have disabilities. He explains that we shouldn't hate these people. On the contrary we should love them. They are people like us; we need to love them and help them. He very much tries to give culture and his expertise to the people.

Disadvantages of Patronage

Although the assistance of patrons is a wonderful short-term boon to needy individuals, many believe that, in the long run, the system perpetuates poverty because patrons generally manipulate the system to maintain their status. It is a co-dependency relationship in which the patron needs people to need him or her. For example, in many parts of the region people complain that an ordinary person without a patron cannot realistically expect justice from the courts. Patrons' gifts keep people emotionally indebted to such a degree that they are unwilling to take action against their benefactors, even while they know their benefactors are, in fact, insuring that the majority of the clients become increasingly needy. The select few who do get ahead substantially due to patronage are expected to return the favor with unquestioning loyalty and blind support for their patrons. Rana said, "There is no one who

There is no one who has money who doesn't use it to keep the position he has.

has money who doesn't use it to keep the position he has." Ammar described sharecropping and perpetual poverty in the Blue Nile state of Sudan. Another Sudanese talked about how mining companies do something similar to sharecropping, putting up the prices in the stores as soon as the workers get paid. Wade said about eighty percent of the Yemeni population lived on loans which they never intended to pay back. If the lender insisted, the borrower would simply take another loan. Even friendship involves loaning money and making one's friend indebted to the lender.

Abu Nader claimed it happens in Lebanon and around the world:

> Okay, where is their wealth? It's become power. They want to keep the people this way so they can go on ruling them. This is a pathetic thing. This goes to damnation wherever you go in the world. Anywhere in the world. It is necessary that we think in a correct manner. Act in a correct manner. See what and where our interests as human beings are.

The pervasive patron-client inequality results in classism and uncritical loyalty to patrons. It colors all social relationships. According to Ram:

> If there isn't a lot of personal benefit, it is hard to show a person respect. For example, if someone wants to marry, he invites the people whose circumstances are good. They have money; maybe they'll bring him a nice gift, come in nice clothes. But the poor, they don't much remember him.

Patronage contributes to the fragmentation of nations into groups loyal to competing patrons, sometimes unthinking loyalty both in political and social settings. Marwan said:

> In Lebanon everything goes into political parties. Now, I'm into parties, but I don't do whatever they tell me or at the hour they want me to go down to the mall, to go down, or the hour they

say you must vote, to vote. That sort of thing. The people don't know how to behave themselves. Continually someone is steering, "Do this and do this and do this." They need to know to do for themselves, how to act, for whom to vote. [People's willingness to engage in destructive behaviors] depends if there is personal advantage or not. If there is personal advantage, "Yeah, let's go!" They go along with him regardless of how right or wrong he is. They want something from him. And the one who doesn't want something, "What is this ignorant person?!"

Ram picked up the same theme regarding Palestine:

[The client gives] loyalty in a negative sense. There is something called submission (*khuḍūʾ*) and there is something called strangling (*khunūʾ*). He [the client] always votes for him [the patron] and speaks well of him, and whatever he [the patron] wants him to do, he does it. Maybe he tells him to jump into a well, and he jumps into a well and doesn't think if it is a good thing. With us it is prohibited to ask, "Why?" Among the politicians it is most common. The ordinary people are not aware. Maybe they will say something in his absence, but in front of the politicians—no! Never! It is prohibited to say anything.

Where a patron-client culture flourishes, so, often, does corruption. Ramy quoted the saying, "Feed a mouth, the eye will be embarrassed." It can be interpreted in two ways, both of which point to difficulties with patronage: 1) Your help humiliates the recipient, and 2) If you feed people, they will close their eyes to whatever else the patron does.

Although comfortable with patronage, Charlie admitted:

Of course there are dangers! Number one: someone like me can abuse that, for personal gain, to fulfill a personal agenda of some sort—position, name . . . that's one. Second, that does not come for free. Usually it's at the expense of someone, and usually it's at the expense of the person who needs the help. I can abuse the needy person and make it at his expense. But I make sure it's at my own expense.

Amjad bemoaned corruption in Iraq:

Everyone tries to use the system. This ministry takes this thing and that ministry takes that. Or the Kurd. Or the Sunni. So what does the Kurd or the Sunni do? Surely he brings a Kurd or a Sunni from his acquaintances, and surely those acquaintances bring acquaintances whom they know. For government projects, they bring people they know, and they take a commission. So maybe I present the project to a specific ministry, but I present a lesser budget, without mentioning the commission. I do the project for less, and keep a very high profit. Certainly the patron profits by the project because he has his relatives and acquaintances.

The Righteous Patron
Interviewees mentioned at least six features of an outstanding patron. The first is *the quantity and quality of the services rendered.* The righteous rich "is generous. So when I had money, I was able to love the people, to help all the people, support all the people—anyone," said Maryam.

Nayla lauded Rafik al-Hariri as both rich and good because of the unique extent of the services he provided:

He was educating children. He built churches, and mosques—he built up both sides. He provided services—a lot. Widows. I have heard that no one knocked on his door and came away empty.

Abu Nader found a certain leader wanting in piety because, in his opinion, he failed to provide the necessary services:

Take, for example, so-and-so. He has money, and the government has money. But the ideas are not getting through to him. There are people with no electricity! He doesn't know. He's told that people don't have electricity and he thinks that the lines have been cut or that there is no fuel. But he doesn't know that there are people lighting a candle and sitting. There are people who cannot study because they haven't got electricity. And there's no water. They are gathering around a spigot outdoors in order to bathe. He doesn't know it. I know it because I've lived it. I've seen people here. Piety is the amount of service you give.

Several of the interviewees were impressed with people doing scientific research for the benefit of all, patrons of humanity. Among them Rana:

You see outside Lebanon people who are doing research, paying their own money to do it. They die poor following the research, but they had a rich life. They get dressed: it doesn't matter to them what they wear. What concerns them is that they did something. Here, no. As long as you have a Rolex watch, and this is Cartier or something, the importance is that you wear something neat.

A second feature of a pious patron, mentioned particularly by the Lebanese, is that he is *not associated with violence or coercion*. According to Zeina: "There are many people who are not candid. They have political parties and weapons, and you don't know how they got their money."

Genuine piety expressed in disinterested benevolence is a third characteristic of a good patron. Abu Nader explains what a pious rich person might look like:

One who has more money and is pious can do more in society. This means that if I have a lot of money, I can put this money or work for the benefit of all. For instance, I can build schools and clinics. I can do good works for the service of the society and those in need.

He contrasts this ideal to the reality, as he sees it, of those who make cheap, meaningless gestures:

> They come up to our area in a big Mercedes like a ghoul, and as soon as there is someone dead, they go and say to the family, "I hope you're adequately taken care of."[506] On what? This one can't make a cup of coffee!

Interviewees judged a patron's sincerity by the degree to which his gifts were given in secret, indiscriminately, and without obvious political or financial advantage for the patron.

A fourth commendable feature of a patron, according to the interviewees, is his *commitment to the good of the whole country*. For Amjad, a good patron stays in the country, even though he has the means to leave, and invests in the future of the nation. Umm Nader, a Shi'ite, wondered about a well-known Sunni,

> Maybe if I went to him tomorrow and told him, "I'm not able to educate my son," or "I'm not able to pay for him to do a specialization," maybe they would help me. Maybe. Or maybe they wouldn't even see me, being that I'm from a [different] denomination or something.

Ahmad firmly believed that al-Hariri benefited the whole nation. He eulogized,

> His entrance into Lebanon . . . raised the country to a new life and he taught the students so that the new generation would not be naïve. He enlightened the world and helped them all to show to the whole world, "This is the face of Lebanon."

Zeina pointed out a fifth praise-worthy feature related to the fourth: *services given are not directly contingent on political loyalty*. Zeina asked rhetorically, "Now, there are people who help, but I don't know. Is it so that they will get a position? Do they say, 'I helped you, now help me get elected,' for example?"

---

[506] Note the striking parallel to James 2:16.

The evangelical interviewees believed strongly that their image has been given a boost through the indiscriminate way in which many Protestant churches offer relief and development services:

> The aid provided by the evangelical church has given the world a good impression. The non-evangelical churches had begun to say that there are people who are distributing aid to exploit the hungry to get them to their churches. This was two or three years ago. Now, the people who are not evangelicals have begun to defend us. They say, "The evangelical church is the only one who has given to us all this time, and never once have they mentioned, 'Come to our church.'" They serve us with only the motive of love. They, who are not evangelicals, have begun to defend the evangelicals. And many of these people were once fighting our church. There are many [other] churches which were bad when it came to this subject. The people have rejected them. There are people who asked us to take their papers and change their legal registration to become evangelicals, because of the behavior of their own denominations and their men of religion toward them.

Sixth, good patrons are characterized by *humility and identification with ordinary people*. Amjad wants a congregation to be able to see in a patron:

> His humility. Not, "I have money, so I give money, and others do the work." No. He might give his time to the church—not just the worship, but other service: preparations, organization, this sort of thing.

Fouad agreed:

> Work. Working with the people. He doesn't come someday to church and see all the people working extra and say, "My only obligation is to pay." No. He works with the people. Humility reflects everything. He returns and is with the people at all of the occasions. He sits with them. His word is always the last, but

he isn't one who forces his opinion on the others. No. He gives opportunity for everyone to speak.

Daoud confirmed Fouad's view, "I agree with him regarding communication. The righteous rich person communicates with the believers, or the people, or his relatives. He goes down with them; he goes down and meets all their needs. He is with them all the time."

Daoud went on to stress the importance of being with people at the time of a death in the family. Lara was also concerned with a humble attitude and special occasions:

Attitude is the way you respect others, listen to others, greet them, don't greet them, visit them, don't visit them, take off your shoes when you visit them, don't take off your shoes when you enter, sit with them in their home, drink a cup of coffee from their cups of coffee. All of these things that don't imply that you feel higher or that you don't feel at ease in their environment. Or if it's someone who is independent of an organization, being generous. So at *eid* you would bring a gift, or clothes for their children, or food. When the baby is born. All of these moments that are celebrated and where the community comes together, you contribute as well. Or when somebody's sick, or when somebody elderly died, you would contribute to the funeral.

Obviously, the fourth, fifth, and sixth qualities listed above demonstrate the influence of modern nation-state, democratic, or egalitarian thinking. They might carry within them seeds of the downfall of the patronage system, because patrons need the loyalty of a core group to remain in power, and people will not give that loyalty unless they perceive the patron is elevated enough to secure an advantage for them.[507] For patrons to remain in power they must be selective in their patronage. A clever patron favors his inner core while dispensing enough services to the rest to win for himself positive relations, if not loyalty. "Patronage cannot easily exist within a democratic state with a central government and an efficient bureaucracy."[508]

---

[507] Kawtharani, "The Interplay," 158.
[508] Moxnes, "Patron-Client Relations," 244.

Abu Nader raised the foundational questions about the legitimacy of the patronage system as a whole. He looked to the West as a model and asked for greater accountability among leaders. Ahmad also looked to the West for models of government which look after the poor in a systematic way. Although he admired al-Hariri greatly, he believed that the former Prime Minister was doing personally what the government should have been doing:

> That is not a responsibility of the rich. But you can't require of every person to do like he does. The government has a duty to help the poor to ensure them the simplest living in order to continue with his life and to lighten the current neglect.

Men of Religion and Patronage

Religious and political patronage often walk hand in hand. The politically ambitious found, contribute to, and use religiously based charitable organizations to further their political goals, and to create an image of piety in the minds of the constituency.[509] Some men of religion exploit the loyalty of their congregations to secure political influence for their own benefit. "Every sheikh, when he has money, pays to become weighty among the people, to become something important," said Rana. There is a widespread and growing sentiment that men of religion and political patronage should be kept as far apart as possible. Consider these quotations:

> I don't think the situation is going to get better and the reason is because we, as Arabs, are convinced that religion is an expert in politics. This is wrong! Religion needs to be by itself and politics by itself so that politics can be successful and the country move on. The country progressed when religion was put to the side (with all respect to religion, whether Muslim or Christian). They put it on the side and they knew their politics, they knew how to do economics, they knew to build from below, to build and expand.

---

[509] Kawtharani, "The Interplay," 51, quoting Johnson, 1986, 46. [Bibliographical material on Johnson was not available to me at the time of writing.] See also Halim Barakat, *The Arab World: Society, Culture and State*, Berkeley: University of California, 1993, 64.

Without noticing that you are Muslim and I am Christian. Egypt will not develop unless they leave religion to the side. (Egypt).

Now, there are two divisions of men of religion. There are men of religion who are Salafists or men of religion only, and there are those in the Islamist movements, like Hamas, and today they are political, like the Muslim Brotherhood. Those ones, the people see them as having a lot of money. They get a lot of support from outside. There are secular politicians and there are Islamist politicians. The Islamist politicians bring big support from outside for the Palestinian people, but they direct all the money just for themselves and the people who are like them—if you hear of Hamas and the Muslim Brotherhood in Gaza. So aid comes to them, very big aid—I'm talking millions—and they burn up this money only on the people who are from them, who are like them. So all the people look to them to get money. They don't sense that they have piety, they sense that, in the end, their goal, their interests, are just money. There are people whose interest is to go to prison, just so that they can get the money. Among the evangelicals, the same thing. They have this perspective that they have leaders who bring aid from outside, and they benefit from the churches. They get a lot of aid and benefit more. Especially the people who combine religion and politics. Many see that they exploit us in order to arrive at their own personal benefit. It's as though they are saying, "They engage in trade using us." Now, this talk you hear from the ordinary evangelical people. But I don't know how reliable this is. Money comes to them, but we don't see much of anything. It all stays theirs. They take us to conferences and this and that, in order for them to benefit.[510] (Palestine)

The view of men of religion has become very negative, that this one has become rich because he is participating in monetary corruption. The religious movements achieved government. Their

---

[510] It is the norm that denominations pay for conferences for their people. The accusation here is of money laundering: clergy hosting conferences to disguise skimming off donations. In fairness, since people are not used to paying for conferences, they frequently and severely underestimate the cost of such an event, so the accusations may be unfounded, as Ram acknowledges.

various divisions are all monetary and belong to the government. (Iraq)

A number of interviewees expressed concern that love of money has eroded the credibility of men of religion who are patrons and has disqualified them as role models and leaders:

> It is certainly inappropriate that men of religion live above the level of the people! How can I imitate the person when he doesn't feel with me? He is telling me to do something which he is unable to do. Their standard of living affects our trust in them, certainly! When you have a sheikh, and he has three, four, five cars, a house, an entourage, or he gets into a position in which he uses his money . . . certainly I am going to be affected. I'm going to stop following that person. (Lebanon)

> The point of view among us about men of religion is not good. In such-and-such a town, the people of the region gave the patriarch a rod of gold. Priceless. The area is full of migrants, and people don't have food. (And he comes on the basis of helping us!) The price of one rod of gold is $100,000. And what does he bring as a gift? He brings for each child a bag in which is a notebook and 2 pens. The people are dying from hunger, and you are giving a rod of gold to the Metropolitan?! Distribute it to the people! So the perspective on men of religion is that they are on one side and the people on another side. They always take everything, and we have to honor them. Without even knowing them, the people have begun to say about men of religion, "That one is a thief and a liar!" Sorry to say it. (Syria)

What Patrons Do

In addition to famous characters, respondents had a great deal to say about the patronage habits of the rich people with whom they were personally acquainted. Many of the acquaintances whom they identified as combining wealth and godliness functioned as patrons or as a combination of patron and friend. Here is a sample of the reasons given:

- "He donated to associations for the needy and those that take care of orphans, as he also helped some of the poor relatives and the people of his village."
- "At feast time he distributed money to the poor."
- "He organized foundations which care for the handicapped and educated the needy."
- "He paid tuition of several young people."
- "He tarred the road to my village."
- "He financed (with others) the purchase of the land for and building of our church, and lots of donations to those in need."
- "He consecrated his money and power to serve whomever seeks him."
- "He helped me go to college by paying my fees."
- "[He is] benevolent, financing welfare projects."
- "He helps people and he offers what is good to everyone in his village."
- "He helped many from the poor class and children in school."
- "He bought a fuel station and distributed diesel fuel for free in his village."
- "They built a basketball court."
- "He gave us a store and a small amount of start-up money."
- "She helps many poor people and helped by paying the hospital fees of many people."
- "Helped the poor people in our village, built things like a playground for people."

An apparently rich person who wishes to be counted as godly in Middle Eastern society will be expected to take on some sort of role as a patron, whether or not aspiring to political office. The patron should be able to expect the loyalty of those to whom he or she provides services, and therefore has the potential to exercise considerable influence.

The ideal patron meets felt needs generously, and this generosity must have some pious foundation evident in a compassionate nature, religious devotion, secrecy in giving, or giving to the needy without sectarian discrimination. There must be no resorting to violence to maintain loyalty. He or she must also be a true patriot and humanitarian who works for the good of the whole nation and of humanity.[511] Patronage can become an evil if the funds for the services are used to manipulate the people, or are embezzled from the public funds.

Patronage and the Bible

Job, as we have seen, presented himself to his friends as the perfect patron in Job 31. Abraham also functioned as a patron to his nephew Lot, showing generosity and making it a matter of honor to protect him and intercede for him. Solomon acted as a patron by feeding large numbers of guests and dependents,[512] stimulating the economy through massive building projects,[513] and funding religious festivals.[514] The Proverbs promote both the generosity and the political astuteness necessary in a good patron.[515] Amos rips into the wealthy of his day for their failure to use their wealth and influence on behalf of the poor, that is, their failure to fulfill the obligations of a patron. The apostles acted as patrons, receiving donations from the rich, organizing to ensure that the monies were fairly distributed

---

[511] And, I would add, such a patron must be a very shrewd politician and distributor of services to convince supporters that they are favored while convincing everyone else that he or she has their good at heart.

[512] 1 Kings 4:22,23. In this case it was patronage of the wealthy, most likely, although verses 20, 21 suggest that everyone got at least some benefit.

[513] 1 Kings 4:26; 5–7; 9:26.

[514] 1 Kings 8:52–66; 9:25.

[515] See the paragraph on patronage in the section on Solomon and the Proverbs, or Proverbs 11:10,11; 11:16,17,24–28; 30;14:24; 16:10–12; 17:26; 19:6; 20:28,29; 22:1; 22:22,23; 24:10–12; 25:23–25; 29:12; 31:8,9,20,23.

among the needy of their community, and receiving the loyalty of their community. Several other positive examples of patronage can be seen in the Bible, among them Joseph,[516] Boaz,[517] Nehemiah,[518] women who followed Jesus,[519] the centurion whose servant Jesus healed,[520] the Apostle Paul,[521] and Phoebe.[522] As a general concept it is not at odds with the Scriptures. On the contrary, in much of the Bible, patrons are portrayed as the noble souls who bring widespread blessing. As Charlie pointed out, "In the Bible the rich used their wealth for the benefit of the ministry and for the growth of personal and communal piety."

However, the Bible shares with some of the interviewees a condemnation of the perversions to which a patronage system is prone. The law rejects patterns which keep people in perpetual poverty. Repeated in many parts of the Scriptures is the prohibition on perverting justice, or gaining wealth and power through violence.[523] Jesus strongly urged benevolence to the needy without discrimination.[524] By teaching that the believer should look for eternal rewards rather than earthly advantage, and by urging anonymous giving, the Lord Jesus demanded that acts of patronage be done for noble, rather than selfish, motives.[525] He himself refused to accept the loyalty of potential clients who wanted to make him a king because he gave them bread.[526]

In his first letter to Timothy, Paul takes pains to point out that all wealthy Christians should fulfill the duties of patrons, without expecting that this will lead to personal gain or guaranteed positions of authority within the community. Under no circumstances is the

---

[516] He served as provider, protector, and mediator for his people (Gen 45; 46:31–47:12; 50:19–21). It is clear that he used his position of power and his wealth to secure the loyalty of his hitherto-unaffectionate siblings and their family, and to promote their welfare. If the Egyptians are to be believed, he was highly successful (Ex 1:1–10).
[517] Ruth 2. The kinsman-redeemer acted as a sort of family patron. See Leviticus 25:25,49.
[518] Nehemiah 5.
[519] Luke 8:1–3.
[520] Luke 7:1–5.
[521] Acts 21:23–26.
[522] Romans 16:1,2.
[523] For example, Deuteronomy 10:17–19; Proverbs 1:8–19; 31:8–9; Isaiah 10:1–3; Micah 6:8–13.
[524] Matthew 5:42.
[525] Matthew 6:1–4; 23:25–28; Luke 22:25–27.
[526] John 6:14,15. The entire chapter cannot be fully understood without the assumption of patronage behind much of what is said.

truth to be compromised in the church's teaching, however influential the potential teacher may be. Leadership roles are to be assigned on the basis of gifts and character. James warns that courting wealthy patrons is dangerous: their protection is not reliable, and the honor they require may mean an unacceptable shunting aside of poor fellow-believers.[527]

Patronage in Practice

The patron-client culture of Middle Eastern countries has tremendous implications for Westerners living in the region. To begin with, regardless of their choice of lifestyle in the Middle East, Westerners have "wealthy connections," and will be expected to help all with whom they associate, using those connections for their advantage. Some of these requests are personal ("Can you get me a visa to America?"), and some related to charitable or religious services ("Will you ask your people in the West to contribute to our project?"). Refusal to attempt to patronize the person in this way will call into question the sincerity of the missionary's friendship or worthiness as an influence in the community. An attempt which ends in failure makes the patron look weak and ineffectual. Repeated occurrences may cause the client to change loyalties and the patron to lose face and influence. Successful attempts build tremendous goodwill.

Of course, this pattern also follows where money is involved. A missionary who represents a Western organization is expected to use that organization to the financial benefit of those he or she influences. Furthermore, Middle Easterners who work for the mission naturally expect that it will use its wealthy connections to further that worker's economic and social status. I know of at least two Western agencies that recruited Middle Eastern believers who, after being hired, expressed anger that the agencies had not bought them Mercedes-Benz cars. Although this is no doubt partially an expression of greed on the part of the Middle Eastern worker, it is also an outworking of the belief that one cannot be respected or effective without money.

---

[527] James 2:1–9. James does not explicitly use the language of patronage here, but it seems clear that those who favor the rich are looking for some benefit. James points out that, in fact, the rich are using their influence *against* the believers (verse 7).

A patron who does not help his client financially does not deserve loyalty, because that patron keeps the client weak and humiliated. Loyalty deserves rewards.

Clearly, a great deal of solid teaching from the Scriptures is necessary to overcome this mindset. Loyalty to God, rather than to a human personality, must be encouraged, and eternal, rather than earthly rewards expected.[528] In addition, diligent pastoral care and personal favors (such as writing a reference for the worker's son's college application) may compensate somewhat for want of economic kick-backs. However, Western leaders should also examine themselves frequently to subtle racism or imperialism which assumes that their Middle Eastern colleagues deserve less than they when it comes to finances, job security, benefits, and titles.

This subtle superiority can surface in a variety of ways. Lara warned, "We need to be conscious of our own motivation, involving people, not thinking we come with all the solutions ready-made, but involving people in the creation of solutions, and recognizing their strengths rather than defining them by their weaknesses."

Loyalty deserves rewards.

We also need to guard against using donations from our organizations to control and manipulate the people to whom we give. Charlie advises, "One other, very important point: giving unconditionally. Some people want to give, but they want to control that gift after it leaves their hands. If they don't control it, they don't give it. God wants us to release, and then the Holy Spirit makes the call." Resentment will arise if too many strings are attached to the money and the recipient feels manipulated. "Money ought never to be used as a power wedge for one part of God's family to enforce its will on other members of God's family."[529]

Sometimes the shoe is on the other foot. Many Christian workers in the Middle East are dependent on churches, institutions, or individuals for support in getting their visas and making needed

---

[528] A theology of divine patronage and its similarities and differences to human patronages would make a fascinating study beyond the scope of this book.
[529] Gary Corwin, "The Root of All Kinds of Confusion" (*Evangelical Missions Quarterly*, vol. 38:1, January 2002): 8.

connections. Westerners tend not to be aware that their sponsors are expending a great deal of time, money, and influence to enable them to stay in the country. Usually the service rendered by the missionary is sufficient to make the local Christian satisfied that the expenditure was worth it, but Westerners should be aware that they may be considered indebted in some fashion: thanks, loyalty, a gift, or some indirect financial return such as getting the mission agency to make an annual donation.

Patronage must be taken into account at all times when we seek to understand the social and power dynamics of a group or organization. In all Middle Eastern churches, the average lay person expects the pastor or priest to act as a patron (and the same is true for other religious leaders). The clergyman is expected to act as representative to the government, employment agency, negotiator, and philanthropist among the people under his care. He is expected to buy from them and use their services faithfully, regardless of the price, relative efficiency, convenience, or quality. Some church members will consider that they are doing the pastor a personal favor by attending or bringing others to church and thus enhancing his sphere of influence. They often expect some sort of service in return.

Given the patron/client mentality, it is to the pastor's advantage if a source of money and other desirables is available from outside the congregation, for five reasons:

1. He is then able to provide services which encourage loyalty to him.
2. He is seen as having wide connections.
3. He is able to enhance his image of wealth or power, and so attract new followers.
4. The enhanced image of the pastor gives his people a sense of collective pride in him as a worthy representative.[530]
5. He is less dependent on his flock, and has leeway to rebuild his support base if followers change loyalties or emigrate.

---

[530] This also applies to titles. I have heard members of the tiny and divided Protestant communities in the region suggest that the Protestant representative to the government be given the title "Patriarch" or "Metropolitan" so as not to appear lesser than his Catholic or Orthodox counterparts.

Some of this may make the missionary cringe, but it is the reality. Biblical teaching is essential, but so is sympathy for the pastor and people enmeshed in this system. It will do no good to criticize without working though what might be some alternatives which are both biblical and doable in the Arab context.

Higher level religious leaders are *de facto* government officials. They have achieved their standings by using their influence for the advantage of their own communities. They are normally well-paid and have substantial "perks." They also face a great deal of rivalry from leaders of other religious groups, and potential supplanters within their own ranks. These leaders can be of tremendous assistance to the missionary, and it is normal Middle Eastern practice to ask for their help. Getting on the wrong side of such a person is dangerous. If the religious leader in question is a person of integrity who genuinely seeks to follow Christ, the best course is to show loyalty and to encourage the leader in his integrity. A great deal of caution is needed in entering into a relationship with a Christian leader whose political and financial ambitions exceed his godliness.

> It will do no good to criticize without working though what might be some alternatives which are both biblical and doable in the Arab context.

The truly godly patron uses his influence to develop rather than merely to give handouts. In addition to economic development, there is a great need for teaching and mentoring. Patrons are ideally poised to give training to people in the wise use of money and in advocacy. They may also be able to effectively challenge the prosperity gospel teaching which has infiltrated parts of the church in the region.

Charlie on Wasṭa and Missionaries

The paradigm that controls all of this is, "It's not what you know, it's who you know." In the Middle East, that's how it works, and that's how you can be effective. I'm able to help a lot of people because of the connections I have. I take a lot of people to dinner. I have a special budget just to take people to dinner. I don't bribe anyone—they know that. I say it up front. I don't break the law for anyone's sake, but I treat people nice. I become their friend. That sometimes translates into becoming the keeper of their secrets and the counselor for their problems. Of course, I give them all these services for nothing. But against that, when I need something, I can pick up the phone and say, "Look, I have an issue with thus-and-so. What should I do?" A lot of times, foreign missionaries are satisfied with living to themselves in the sense that when they aren't doing ministry, they're secluded from the community, and they fail to build a network of friends outside the realm of Christian believers, and they fail to build a network of people they can go to in time of trouble. A by-product of these connections is the opportunities I get to share the gospel. I can't tell you. I have a friend in high places who helps me in my ministry. Missionaries need to reach out to the community, visit people, invite people to their homes. You make connections for the sake of those who have no voice, no connection.

I'm point B between point A and point C. It's not between below and above. It's between one point and another. I'm right in the middle. It's a very good relationship because I'm always listening to their needs and trying to help and support. It has to do with my attitude, whether I want to show an air of superiority or say, "Hey, the Lord placed me in this position, just like Joseph, just like Daniel, to help the people of God. I'm just serving the Lord."

There is a price. When I take people out, I'm paying! And you know how the Lebanese are. Monday night I had a dinner. I had to invite someone very high up in government who's been my friend for years now. I promise you I'm not taking him to McDonald's! But the help this lady has given me has been immeasurable. I can use that for my own advantage at the expense of the little man, or I can serve the little man at my own expense, and have an opportunity to share the gospel with this individual high up in the ranks.

> What are my expectations from the recipients? Zero. Nothing. I don't expect a thing. I don't even expect them to come to church. Our policy in relief has nothing to do with whether they come to church. If they're needy, they're going to get help. If I have the ability. If they come to church, hallelujah, glory! We love them. And this is a constant message. In our work with refugees, we hammer this. "We love you. We don't look down on you. We know that circumstances have been hard on you, but we want you to know here's a shoulder to cry on, a corner we can pray for your need." And that's exactly what we do. And the beauty of it now is there's a group of the refugees who've been saved and baptized who pray for each other. We try to treat them on par. When we go up to our church camp every year, we invite no less than 20 people, fully covered from the church, to attend our church camp and be part of the camp. We pay for transportation, accommodation, and food.

Protestant churches have found that their emphasis on the priesthood of all believers has in practice led to a great deal of division around the world. The ideals of patronage compound the problem. In hierarchical systems of church government, there are some safeguards which prevent disloyalty to leaders above one's own level. Among Protestants in the Middle East, anyone with a little ambition can solicit funds from the West or from influential Middle Easterners and start their own church, ministry, seminary, or mission. Competition for loyal followers is sometimes intense among pastors and other leaders. To cement loyalty, pastors often emphasize denominational loyalty and distinctives at the expense of loyalty to the kingdom of God. Missionaries have a unique contribution to make in reminding leaders and people that they are part of a greater whole, and that all true believers are on the same team. We need to guard against allowing ourselves and our financial connections to be used to further divide Christ's body. Nor should our money go to siphon the best national workers away from local organizations to support our projects.[531]

Workers from wealthy Western nations also need to be careful that they do not contribute to a sense of dependency and helplessness among church leaders and people when it comes to mission. If we consider mission impossible or inferior unless it has all of the apparatus to which Western missionaries are accustomed, then we set the financial bar too high for the Middle Easterner to reach without our patronage, and the emotional ownership of the work remains with the patron.[532]

Maya and Ramy, themselves Syrians, worked with Syrian refugees. They were ready with advice for outsiders: "Don't believe the people. Westerners are too trusting." Ramy added, "Our people are not satisfied. No matter how much you give it will not be enough. The word 'needy' is very broad, and all will say it." Glades warned against a sense of entitlement that people feel because they have suffered from the war. Misho chipped in, "Once you give people something once or twice, they come to see it as their right on a permanent basis."

One of the problems with patronage from afar is that it is difficult to form a reciprocal relationship, especially if there is no direct personal contact between patron and client. If possible, large donations or regular support from an overseas patron to a Middle Eastern client should be accompanied by visits which will allow a relationship to form, bring a degree of accountability, and offer a chance of reciprocity.[533] A Christ-like patron will never be content with the mere giving of money, but will be engaged in practical ministries for and alongside their clients: cleaning, setting up chairs, attending meetings, sharing in the planning and administration of community events, and being with people at the most important moments of their lives.

---

[531] Bernard T. Adeney, *Strange Virtues: Ethics in a Multicultural World* (Leicester: Apollos, 1995), 161.
[532] David J. Bosch, *Transforming Mission: Paradigm Shifts in Theology of Mission* (Maryknoll: Orbis, 1991), 295–296.
[533] *Evangelism and Social Responsibility: An Evangelical Commitment*, No. 21 Grand Rapids Report (Grand Rapids: Lausanne Committee for World Evangelization and the World Evangelical Fellowship, 1982), 55–56.

Sometimes clients move from gratitude to ingratiation, even attempting to kiss one's hand. Lara suggested that patrons brush off thanks when it starts to become too effusive. She would tell the overly grateful, "You're a client coming for this service and it's my job to serve you. Enough!"

Inherent in the patronage system is a lack of accountability in the management of the treasuries of government offices and charitable organizations. Audits bespeak mistrust, and patrons demand loyalty. Clients want their patron to be free to divert funds for their benefit, and fear that those benefits will be cut off if they ask too many questions. This results, for most Middle Eastern governments, in staggering debt.[534] Money disappears in huge quantities, and politicians, bureaucrats, and their friends become fabulously wealthy. The same thing can happen in the church. I know of at least three cases within the evangelical church in Lebanon of embezzlement of tens of thousands of dollars. The apostles allowed themselves to be held accountable by the believers,[535] but many Middle Eastern clergy are accountable to no one on earth. It makes sense to me in such circumstances to work firmly but tactfully toward transparency in financial management, and toward giving extra honor and authority to those leaders who are able to demonstrate their integrity on paper.[536]

I have sometimes heard those engaged in church planting pipe-dreaming of the new-style church which will someday be born innocent of the corruption and divisiveness which pervade the Christian-background churches of the region. A truly indigenous church will have to deal with patronage issues every bit as thorny as the rest of the Middle Eastern Church faces. Further, for a church to

---

[534] In Lebanon for example, "Debt servicing consumes 45% of the GNP . . . Public debt [is] 140% of GNP." Patrick Johnstone and Jason Mandryk, *Operation World* (Paternoster Lifestyle, 2001), 399.
[535] Acts 6:1–6. See also 2 Corinthians 8:19–21.
[536] I recall a discussion with two Lebanese visitors to the English-speaking Anglican church in Beirut. The first was appalled to see that the offering was counted in the front of the sanctuary by two members directly after the meeting. "They don't trust one another!" she said. The second Lebanese person was impressed by this accountability arrangement, and wished aloud that it could be applied to the priest in his village.

be truly indigenous, it will need to be headed by a patron/patriarch[537] who has influence over and loyalty from others. I have heard it suggested[538] that potential patrons be the focus of evangelism, and this makes sense. However, such a person would need to be truly converted, for he or she stands to lose more than others by following Christ. It is hard for a rich person to enter the kingdom of heaven.

When a Middle Easterner needs help, he or she does not usually go to just any rich or powerful person, but to the person to whom he or she feels greatest loyalty and affiliation. When a Christian expatriate worker faces a crisis, Middle Eastern onlookers will surmise a great deal based on the person to whom the worker goes for assistance. For workers who have connections with local Christian leaders, it is probably best to look to them first, rather than to an embassy. Workers whose case is advocated by the embassy may find themselves in the mind of local people entwined with the politics of that embassy.

Ram's advice to missionaries:

> Try to fulfill a need more than merely giving money. So for instance, I find an elderly man who needs a bed, I buy him a bed. I enter into their lives. I speak with them about their need. Mostly I speak with them rather than giving them the money. Maybe they will spend it on something wrong. Or maybe he will look at me as dollars. I love you and I sense that you have this problem, so I bring you this bed, or this washing machine, or . . . Here you will know that I have love for you, not that I want to spend on you. And this makes you feel related.

Ram's advice was far and away the majority view, but Lara cautioned against a condescending attitude that we patrons know better than the recipients what they need or that we are wiser in our use of money given for their sake than they are.

---

[537] As the common linguistic roots indicate, patronage is closely related to patriarchy in Arab societies. For the pervasive role of the patriarch at all levels of society, see Sharabi, Hisham, "The Dialectics of Patriarchy in Arab Society," In *Arab Society*, ed. Samih K. Farsoun (London: Croom Helm, 1985), 81–98.

[538] Among others, by Greg Livingstone in his book, *Planting Churches in Muslim Cities: A Team Approach*, (Grand Rapids: Baker, 1993), 121.

Middle Easterners are cynical about motives for charitable giving, especially when the giving is done by someone representing another religious group. To some Muslims I know personally, Christian charity work is an attempt at political and religious imperialism. If it is given only to those who profess Christ, it is called buying converts. If it is given without discrimination in Muslim areas, it is seen as buying influence. I have heard both Christians and Muslims accuse one another of buying converts and using money in manipulative ways. While it is impossible to escape false accusations, it is wise to avoid unnecessary provocation. Financial gifts quietly given by individuals in the context of long-term friendship seem more genuine than public donations from programs staffed by outsiders. Anything that smacks of manipulation should be particularly avoided, such as making gifts or services contingent upon attendance at religious meetings.

Middle Easterners of the middle and lower classes respect a wealthy person who finds the time to meet their needs. Jonathan Bonk points out:

> . . . the importance of practicing a missiology of the neighbor. This simply means deliberately allowing a poor person to use us to fulfill their personal dreams and meet their personal needs. Is it not remarkable that we know more about the interruptions in Jesus' busy schedule than we know about anything else he said or did? Jesus, whose task it was to save the world, was constantly interrupted by a steady stream of persons whose agendas were intensely personal. He stopped what he was doing to pay attention to ordinary, very needy persons—the blind, leprous, sick, accused, or marginalized—taking their personal agendas seriously enough to interrupt what he was doing, to do what they wanted him to do. Missionaries today can do no less, even if the people who came to them simply want a better, more secure way of life with more hopeful opportunities for themselves and their children. If this is how God worked to save the world, it is still how he works through his servants to disciple the nations. The only *a priori* agenda to

which a missionary is bound is to love God with all his/her heart, and his/her neighbor as himself.[539]

By so living, the missionary provides a living model of the message of the gospel that God is a great patron and that Jesus is the wasīṭ who puts us in relationship with God.[540]

---

[539] Jonathan Bonk, "Toward Common Sense Missiology" (2002), 23.
[540] Moxnes, "Patron-Client Relations," (1991), 257–260.

Epilogue

Money and righteousness are hot topics on God's agenda, if the number of times they are addressed in the Scriptures is any indication. They are also crucial topics in the minds of many Middle Easterners. Western culture, however, often considers finances and piety to be personal issues not appropriate for discussion. As Christian workers in the Middle East, we *must* discuss the issues or we will dull the edge of our effectiveness. More importantly, we must listen to what the people we claim to serve are saying about the wealth we enjoy. Then the real work begins: making daily choices about money that bear witness to the righteousness of God among the people of the Middle East.

Glossary

Halal: permissible in Islamic law.

Haram: forbidden in Islamic law.

Iftar: the meal with which the fast is broken at sundown.

MBB: abbreviation for "Muslim-background Believer," a believer in Christ from a Muslim background.

Power distance: the degree to which the less powerful members of a society accept and expect that power is distributed unequally.[541]

Qat: a stimulant used widely as a socially-acceptable drug in Yemen.

Wāsta: the influence of a well-connected intermediary.

Wasīṭ: an intermediary, one who using his or her personal connections on behalf of another.

---

[541] Geert Hofstede, "Dimensions of National Culture," on line at www.geert-hofstede.com/national-culture.html. Accessed 18 September 2017.

Bibliography

Adeney, Bernard T. *Strange Virtues: Ethics in a Multicultural World.* Leicester: Apollos, 1995.

Adeney, Miriam and Sadiri Joy Tira. *Wealth, Women and God: How to Flourish Spiritually and Economically In Tough Places.* Manila: Lifechange, 2014.

Albright, W. F. and C. S. Mann. *Matthew.* From *The Anchor Bible* series. W. F. Albright and D. N. Freedman, editors. Garden City, New York: Doubleday, 1971.

Andersen, Francis I. *Job: An Introduction and Commentary.* Downer's Grove: IVP, 1976.

Barrett, David, George T. Kurian, and Todd M. Johnson. *The World Christian Encyclopedia,* vol. 2. Oxford: Oxford Press, 2001, s.v. "Lebanon."

Barakat, Halim. *The Arab World: Society, Culture and State.* Berkeley: University of California, 1993.

Bassler, Jouette M. *God & Money: Asking for Money in the New Testament.* Nashville: Abingdon, 1991.

Berko, Roy M., Andrew D. Wolvin, and Darlyn R. Wolvin. *Communicating: A Social and Career Focus,* 4th ed. Boston: Houghton Mifflin, 1989.

Bonk, Jonathan J. *Missions and Money: Affluence as a Western Missionary Problem.* Maryknoll: Orbis, 1991.

Bonk, Jonathan J. "Toward Common Sense Missiology: A Response." *Evangelical Missions Quarterly,* 38:1 (2002), 22–23.

Bosch, David J. *Transforming Mission: Paradigm Shifts in Theology of Mission.* Maryknoll: Orbis, 1991.

Chartouni, Charles E. *Conflict Resolution in Lebanon: Myth and Reality.* n.p: Foundation for Human and Humanitarian Rights (Lebanon), n.d.

Clouse, Robert G. editor. *Wealth and Poverty: Four Christian Views of Economics.* Downers Grove: Intervarsity, 1984.

Corwin, Gary. "The Root of All Kinds of Confusion." *Evangelical Missions Quarterly, 38:1,* January, 2002.

Countryman, L. Wm. *The Rich Christian in the Church of the Early Empire: Contradictions and Accommodations.* New York: Edwin Mellen Press, 1980.

Cragg, Kenneth. "The Riddle of Man and the Silence of God: A Christian Perception of Muslim Response." *International Bulletin of Missionary Research,* vol. 17, #4, October 1993, 160–163.

"Demographics of Lebanon." *Abacci Atlas.* <http://www.abacci.com/atlas/demography.asp?countryID=247>.

Delitzsch, F. *Proverbs, Ecclesiastes, Song of Solomon, vol. VI, Commentary on the Old Testament in Ten Volumes* by C. F. Keil and F. Delitzsch, trans. James Martin. Grand Rapids: Eerdmans, 1980.

Dib, Kamal. "A Strategy to Investigate Lebanese Corruption and Debt." *The Daily Star,* 14 June 2005, 11.

Douglas, J. D., *et al,* editors. *The Illustrated Bible Dictionary.* Leicester: IVP, 1980.

Devito, Joseph A. *Human Communication: The Basic Course.* New York: Longman, 1997.

Dunn, James D. G. and Alan M. Suggate. *The Justice of God: A Fresh Look at the Old Doctrine of Justification by Faith.* Grand Rapids: Eerdmans, 1993.

"Encyclopedia: Demographics of Lebanon." *nationmaster.com.* <http://www.nationmaster.com/encyclopedia/Demographics-of-Lebanon>.

Evangelism and Social Responsibility: An Evangelical Commitment, No. 21 Grand Rapids Report. Grand Rapids: Lausanne Committee for World Evangelization and the World Evangelical Fellowship, 1982.

Fetterman, David M. *Ethnography: Step by Step (Applied Social Research Methods),* 2nd edition. Thousand Oaks, California: Sage, 1998.

Foster, Richard. *Celebration of Discipline: The Path to Spiritual Growth.* New York: Harper and Row, 1978.

Hamd, Robert. *Migrant Domestic Workers, The Church, and Mission.* (Doctoral dissertation). Ann Arbor: ProQuest, 2012.

Hammersley, Martyn and Paul Atkinson. *Ethnography: Principles and Practice.* London: Routledge, 1983.

Hare, Douglas R. A. *Matthew. From Interpretation: A Bible Commentary for Teaching and Preaching* series, James Luther Mays, editor. Louisville: Knox, 1993.

Harrison, Roland Kenneth. *Introduction to the Old Testament.* Grand Rapids: Eerdmans, 1969.

Hartley, John E. *The Book of Job.* Grand Rapids: Eerdmans, 1988.

Hill, David. *The Gospel of Matthew.* From *The New Century Bible Commentary* series. Grand Rapids; Eerdmans, 1972.

Hofstede, Geert. *Cultures and Organizations: Software of the Mind.* London: McGraw-Hill, 1991.

Hofstede, Geert. "Dimensions of National Culture," on line at www.geert-hofstede.com/national-culture.html. Accessed 18 September 2017.

Hunter, Archibald M. *A Pattern for Life: An Exposition of the Sermon on the Mount*, revised ed. Philadelphia: Westminster, 1965.

Jeremias, Joachim. *Jerusalem in the Time of Jesus*. Philadelphia: Fortress, 1969.

Johnstone, Patrick, and Jason Mandryk. *Operation World*, 21st Century ed. Waynesboro, GA: Paternoster Lifestyle, 2001.

Judge, E. A. *The Social Pattern of Christian Groups in the First Century*. London: Tyndale, 1960.

Kidd, Reggie M. *Wealth and Beneficence in the Pastoral Epistles: A "Bourgeois" Form of Early Christianity?* Atlanta: Scholars Press, 1990.

Koenig, John. *New Testament Hospitality: Partnership with Strangers as Promise and Mission*. Philadelphia: Fortress, 1985.

Lebanon's Geography, <http://www.ghazi.de/populat.html>.

Lingenfelter, Sherwood. *Transforming Culture: A Challenge for Christian Mission*, 2nd ed. Grand Rapids: Baker, 1998.

Livingstone, Greg. *Planting Churches in Muslim Cities: A Team Approach*. Grand Rapids: Baker, 1993.

Mallat, Chibli. *Shi'i Thought from the South of Lebanon (Papers on Lebanon #7)*. Oxford: Centre for Lebanese Studies, 1988.

Mallouhi, Christine A. *Miniskirts, Mothers & Muslims: A Christian Woman in a Muslim Land*. Oxford: Monarch, 2004.

Mar Osthathios, Geevarghese. "Mission in the Context of Endemic Poverty and in Situations of Affluence." Place, publisher, and date unavailable.

Meeks, Wayne A. *The First Urban Christians: The Social World of the Apostle Paul*. New Haven: Yale, 1983.

Meyer, F. B. *Inherit the Kingdom: The Sermon on the Mount*. Wheaton: Victor, 1904.

Moxnes, Halvar. "Patron-Client Relations and the New Community in Luke-Acts. In *The Social World of Luke-Acts: Models for Interpretation*, Jerome H. Neyrey, editor. Peabody, MA: Hendrickson, 1991, 241–270.

North, Gary. "A Free Market Response." In *Wealth and Poverty: Four Christian Views of Economics*, edited by Robert G. Clouse. Downers Grove: Intervarsity, 1984.

Oakman, Douglas E. "The Countryside in Luke-Acts." In *The Social World of Luke-Acts: Models for Interpretation*. Neyrey, Jerome H., editor. Peabody, MA: Hendrickson, 1991.

Patai, Raphael. *The Arab Mind*. New York: Charles Scribner's Sons, 1973.

Sharabi, Hisham. 1985. "The Dialectics of Patriarchy in Arab Society." In *Arab Society*, ed. Samih K. Farsoun, 81–98. London: Croom Helm.

Sider, Ronald J. *Rich Christians in an Age of Hunger: A Biblical Study.* Downers Grove: Intervarsity, 1980.

Simply Communicate. Bangalore: TAFTEE, no date.

Stott, John R. W. *Christian Counter Culture: The Message of the Sermon on the Mount.* Downers Grove: Intervarsity, 1978.

Stuart, Douglas. *Old Testament Exegesis: A Primer for Students and Pastors, 2nd ed.* Philadelphia: Westminster, 1980.

Thomas, Jim. *Doing Critical Ethnography (Qualitative Research Methods, vol. 26).* Newbury Park, California: Sage, 1993.

Wheeler, Sondra Ely. *Wealth as Peril and Obligation: The New Testament on Possessions.* Grand Rapids: Eerdmans, 1995.

www.ingramcontent.com/pod-product-compliance
Ingram Content Group UK Ltd.
Pitfield, Milton Keynes, MK11 3LW, UK
UKHW022239230426
12048UKWH00018BA/1348